Michael T. Battista

COGNITION-BASED ASSESSMENT & TEACHING

of Fractions

Building on Students' Reasoning

HEINEMANN
Portsmouth, NH

Heinemann
361 Hanover Street
Portsmouth, NH 03801–3912
www.heinemann.com

Offices and agents throughout the world

Library of Congress Cataloging-in-Publication Data
Battista, Michael T.
    Cognition-based assessment and teaching of fractions : building on students' reasoning / Michael Battista.
        p. cm.
    Includes bibliographical references.
    ISBN-13: 978-0-325-04345-6
    ISBN-10: 0-325-04345-0
    1. Fractions—Study and teaching (Elementary).   2. Cognitive learning.   I. Title.
QA137.B37 2012
513.2'607—dc23   2011048484

Editor: Katherine Bryant
Production: Victoria Merecki
Interior and cover designs: Monica Crigler
Typesetter: Publishers' Design & Production Services, Inc.
Website developer: Nicole Russell
Manufacturing: Steve Bernier

Printed in the United States of America on acid-free paper

21 20 19 18   VP   6 7 8 9

Contents

Acknowledgments

I would like to thank the numerous students, parents, teachers, school districts, and research assistants who participated in the CBA project.

I especially want to thank Kathy Battista who has provided invaluable advice and work throughout the CBA project.

Research and development efforts for CBA were supported in part by the National Science Foundation under Grant numbers 0099047, 0352898, 554470, 838137. The opinions, findings, conclusions, and recommendations, however, are those of the author and do not necessarily reflect the views of the National Science Foundation.

—*Michael Battista*

Introduction

Traditional mathematics instruction requires all students to learn a fixed curriculum at the same pace and in the same way. At any point in traditional curricula, instruction *assumes* that students have already mastered earlier content and, based on that assumption, specifies what and how students should learn next. The sequence of lessons is fixed; there is little flexibility to meet individual students' learning needs. Although this approach appears to work for the top 20 percent of students, it does not work for the other 80 percent (Battista 1999, 2001). And even for the top 20 percent of students, the traditional approach is not maximally effective (Battista 1999, 2001). For many students, traditional instruction is so distant from their needs that each day they make little or no learning progress and fall farther and farther behind curriculum demands. In contrast, Cognition-Based Assessment (CBA) offers a cognition-based, needs-sensitive framework to support teaching that enables *all* students to understand, make personal sense of, and become proficient with mathematics.

The CBA approach to teaching mathematics focuses on deep understanding and reasoning, within the context of continually assessing and understanding students' mathematical thinking, then building on that thinking instructionally. Rather than teaching predetermined, fixed content at times when it is inaccessible to many students, the CBA approach focuses on maximizing *individual student progress, no matter where students are in their personal development*. As a result, you can move your students toward reasonable, grade-level learning benchmarks in maximally effective ways. Designed to work with any curriculum, CBA will enable you to better understand and respond to your students' learning needs and help you choose instructional activities that are best for your students.

There are six books in the CBA project:

- *Cognition-Based Assessment and Teaching of Place Value*
- *Cognition-Based Assessment and Teaching of Addition and Subtraction*
- *Cognition-Based Assessment and Teaching of Multiplication and Division*
- *Cognition-Based Assessment and Teaching of Fractions*
- *Cognition-Based Assessment and Teaching of Geometric Shapes*
- *Cognition-Based Assessment and Teaching of Geometric Measurement*

Any of these books can be used independently, though you may find it helpful to refer to several because the topics covered are interrelated.

Critical Components of CBA

The CBA approach emphasizes three key components that support students' mathematical sense making and proficiency:

- clear, coherent, and organized research-based descriptions of students' development of meaning for core ideas and reasoning processes in elementary school mathematics;
- assessment tasks that determine how each of student is reasoning about these ideas; and
- detailed descriptions of the kinds of instructional activities that will help students at each level of reasoning about these ideas.

More specifically, CBA includes the following essential components.

Levels of Sophistication in Student Reasoning

For many mathematical topics, researchers have found that students' development of mathematical conceptualizations and reasoning can be characterized in terms of "levels of sophistication" (Battista, 2004; Battista and Clements, 1996; Battista et al., 1998; Cobb and Wheatley, 1988; Fuson et al., 1997; Steffe, 1988, 1992; van Hiele, 1986). Chapter 2 provides a framework that describes the development of students' thinking and learning about fractions in terms of such levels. This framework describes the "cognitive terrain" in which students' learning trajectories occur, including:

- the levels of sophistication that students pass through in moving from their intuitive ideas and reasoning to a more formal understanding of mathematical concepts;
- cognitive obstacles that students face in learning; and
- fundamental mental processes that underlie concept development and reasoning.

Figure 1 sketches the cognitive terrain that students must ascend to attain understanding of fractions. This terrain starts with students' preinstructional reasoning about fractions, ends with a formal and deep understanding of fractions, and indicates the cognitive plateaus reached by students along the way. Not pictured in the sketch are sublevels of understanding that may exist at each plateau level. Note that students may travel slightly different trajectories in ascending through this cognitive terrain, and they may end their trajectories at different places, depending on the curricula and teaching they experience.

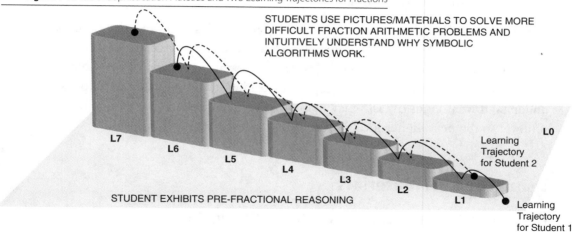

Figure 1 Levels of Sophistication Plateaus and Two Learning Trajectories for Fractions

STUDENTS USE PICTURES/MATERIALS TO SOLVE MORE DIFFICULT FRACTION ARITHMETIC PROBLEMS AND INTUITIVELY UNDERSTAND WHY SYMBOLIC ALGORITHMS WORK.

L7 L6 L5 L4 L3 L2 L1 L0

Learning Trajectory for Student 2

Learning Trajectory for Student 1

STUDENT EXHIBITS PRE-FRACTIONAL REASONING

A Note About Student Work Samples

Chapter 2 includes many examples of students' work, which are invaluable for understanding and using the levels. All of these examples are important because they show the rich diversity of student thinking at each level. However, the first time you work through the materials, you may want to read only a few examples for each type of reasoning—just enough examples to comprehend the basic idea of the level. Later, as you use the assessment tasks and instructional activities with your students, you can sharpen your understanding by examining additional examples both in the level descriptions and in the level examples for each assessment task.

Assessment Tasks

The Appendix contains a set of CBA assessment tasks that will enable you to determine your students' mathematical thinking and precisely locate students' positions in the cognitive terrain for learning fractions. These tasks not only assess exactly what students can do, but they reveal students' reasoning and underlying mathematical cognitions. The tasks are followed by a description of what each level of reasoning might look like for each assessment task. These descriptions will help you pinpoint your students' positions in the cognitive terrain of learning.

Using CBA assessment tasks to determine which levels of reasoning students are using will help you pinpoint students' learning progress, know where students should proceed next in constructing meaning and competence for the idea, and decide which instructional activities will best promote students' movement to higher levels of reasoning. It can also help guide your questions and responses in classroom discussions and in students' small-group work. The CBA website at www.heinemann .com/products/E04345.aspx includes additional assessment tasks that you can use to further investigate your students' understanding of fractions.

Instructional Suggestions

Chapter 3 provides suggestions for instructional activities that can help students progress to higher levels of reasoning. These activities are designed to meet the needs of students at each CBA level. The instructional suggestions are not meant to be comprehensive treatments of topics. Instead, they are intended to help you understand what kinds of tasks may help students make progress from one level or sublevel to the next higher level or sublevel.

Using the CBA Materials

Determining Students' Levels of Sophistication

You can use CBA assessment tasks in several ways to determine students' levels of sophistication in reasoning about fractions.

Individual Interviews

The most accurate way to determine students' levels of sophistication is to administer the CBA assessment tasks in individual interviews with students.[1] For many students, interviews make describing their thinking much easier—they are perfectly capable of describing their thinking orally but have difficulty doing it in writing. Individual interviews also enable teachers to ask probing questions at just the right time, which can be extremely helpful in revealing students' thinking. (Beyond assessment purposes, the individual attention that students receive in individual assessment interviews provides students with added motivation, engagement, and learning.)

Whole-Class Discussion

In an "embedded assessment" model—in which assessment is embedded within instruction—you can give an assessment task to your whole class as an instructional activity. Each student should have a student sheet with the task on it. Students do all their work on their student sheets and describe in writing how they solve the task. When all the students have finished writing their descriptions of their solution methods, lead a class discussion of those methods. For instance, many teachers have a number of individual students present their solutions on an overhead projector or a document-projection device. As students describe their thinking, ask questions that encourage students to provide the detail you need to determine what levels of reasoning they are using. Also, at times, you can repeat or summarize students' thinking in ways that model good explanations (but be sure to provide accurate

---

[1] For helpful advice on scheduling and conducting student interviews, see Buschman (2001).

descriptions of what students say instead of formal versions of their reasoning). After each different student explanation, you can ask how many students used the strategy described. It is important that you not only have students orally describe their solution strategies but that you talk about how they can write and represent their strategies on paper. For instance, after a student has orally described his strategy, ask the class, "How could you describe this strategy on paper so that I would understand it without being able to talk to you?"

Another way to see if students' written descriptions accurately describe their solution strategies is to ask students to come up to your desk and tell you individually what they did, which you can then compare to what they wrote.

Individual and Small-Group Work

You can also determine the nature of students' reasoning by circulating around the room as students are working individually or in small groups on CBA assessment tasks or instructional activities. Observe student strategies and ask students to describe what they are doing as they are doing it. Seeing students actually work on problems often provides more accurate insights into what they are doing and thinking than merely hearing their explanations of their completed solutions (which sometimes do not match what they did). Also, as you talk to and observe students during individual or small-group problem solving, for students who are having difficulty accurately describing their work, write notes to yourself on students' papers that tell you what they said and did (these notes are descriptive, not evaluative).

The Importance of Questioning

Keep in mind that the more students describe their thinking, the better they will become at describing that thinking, especially if you guide them toward providing increasingly accurate and detailed descriptions of their reasoning. For instance, consider a student working on the problem, "What is 1/2 + 1/3?" Suppose Jim writes "1/2 + 1/3 = 2/5" as his explanation of his strategy. Ask additional questions.

Teacher: *What did you do to figure out that 1/2 + 1/3 = 2/5?*

Jim: *I added.*

Teacher: *How did you add—show me.*

Jim: *I put 2 on the top and 5 on the bottom.*

Teacher: *How did you get your answer? Show me how you thought about this problem.*

Jim: *I drew pictures.*

Teacher: *Show me your pictures and what you did with them.*

Jim: *I drew the fractions.*

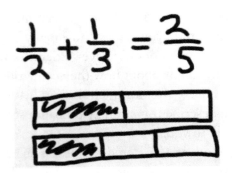

Teacher: *Good. Explain how the picture showed you that the answer is 2/5.*

Jim: *There are 5 parts and 2 are shaded, that's 2/5.*

Teacher: *So on your paper, show your picture and write what you said about how the picture showed 2/5.*

Listed below are some questions that can be helpful in conducting individual interviews, interacting with students during small-group work, or conducting a classroom discussion of an assessment task:

- That's interesting; tell me what you did.
- Tell me how you found your answer.
- How did you figure out this problem?
- I'd really like to understand how you're thinking; can you tell me more about it?
- Why did you do that?
- What were you thinking when you moved these objects?
- Did you check your answer to see whether it is correct? How?
- Explain your drawing to me.
- What do these marks that you made mean?
- What were you thinking when you did this part of the problem?
- What do you mean when you say . . . ?

Monitoring the Development of Students' Reasoning

The CBA materials are designed to help you assess levels of reasoning, not levels of students. Indeed, a student might use different levels of reasoning on different tasks. For instance, a student might operate at a higher level when using physical materials such as place-value blocks than when she does not have physical materials to support her thinking. Also, a student might operate at different levels on tasks that are familiar to her, or that she has practiced, as opposed to tasks that are totally new to her. So, rather than attempting to assign a single level to a student, you should analyze a student's reasoning on several assessment tasks, then develop an overall profile of how she is reasoning about the topic. An example of how this is done appears in Chapter 2.

To carefully monitor and even report to parents the development of student reasoning about particular mathematical topics, many teachers keep detailed records of students' CBA reasoning levels during the school year. To do this, choose several CBA assessment tasks for each major mathematical topic you will cover during the year. Administer these tasks to all of your students either as individual interviews or as written work at several different times during the school year (for example, before and after each curriculum unit dealing with the topic). In addition to noting the tasks used and the date, record what levels each student used on the tasks.

Differentiating Instruction to Meet Individual Students' Learning Needs

You can tailor instruction to meet individual students' learning needs in several ways.

Individualized Instruction

The most effective way is to work with students individually, using the levels and tasks to precisely assess and guide students' learning. This approach is an extremely powerful way to maximize an individual student's learning.

Instruction by CBA Groups

Another effective way of meeting students' needs is by putting students into groups based on their CBA levels of reasoning about a mathematical topic. You can then look to the instructional suggestions for tasks that will be maximally effective for helping the students in each group. For instance, you might have three or four groups in your class, each consisting of students who are reasoning at about the same CBA levels and need the same type of instruction.

Whole-Class Instruction

Another approach that many teachers have used successfully is selecting sets of tasks that all students in a class can benefit from doing. You do this by first determining the different levels of reasoning among students in the class. Then, as you consider possible instructional tasks, ask yourself these questions:

- "How will students at each level of reasoning attempt to do this task?"
- "Can students at different levels of reasoning *succeed* on the task by using different strategies?" (Avoid tasks that some students will not have any way of completing successfully.)
- "How will students at each level benefit by doing the task?"

▦ "Will seeing how different students do the task help other students progress to higher levels of thinking because they are ready to hear new ways of reasoning about the task?"

Also, sets of tasks can be sequenced so that initial problems target students using lower levels of reasoning while later tasks target students using higher levels.

Another way to individualize whole-class instruction is to ask different questions to students at different levels as you circulate among students working in small groups. For instance, for students who use unequal pieces in determining fractions, you might ask, When you tried to find 1/3, did you divide the cake into 3 equal pieces? If we share the pieces for 3 people, will each person get the same amount of cake? Knowledge of CBA levels is invaluable in devising good questions and in asking appropriate questions for different students. In fact, when preparing to teach a lesson, many teachers use levels-of-sophistication descriptions to think about the kinds of questions they will ask students who are functioning at different levels.

Choosing which students to put into small groups for whole-class inquiry-based instruction is also important. If you think of your students' CBA levels of reasoning on a particular type of task as being divided into three groups, you might put students in the high and middle groups together, or students in the middle and low groups together. Generally, putting students in the high and low groups together is not effective because their thinking is likely to be too different.

Assessment and Accountability

As a consequence of state and federal testing and accountability initiatives, most school districts and teachers are looking for materials and methods that will help them achieve state performance benchmarks. CBA is a powerful tool that can help you help your students achieve these benchmarks by:

▦ monitoring students' development of reasoning about core mathematical ideas;

▦ identifying students who are having difficulties learning these ideas and diagnosing the nature of these difficulties;

▦ understanding the nature of weaknesses identified by annual state mathematics assessments results *along with causes for these weaknesses*; and

▦ understanding a framework for remediating student difficulties in conceptually and cognitively sound ways.

Moving Beyond Deficit Models

The CBA materials can help you move beyond the "deficit" model of traditional diagnosis and remediation. In the deficit model, teachers wait until students fail before attempting to diagnose and remediate their learning problems. CBA offers a more powerful, preventative model for helping students. By using CBA materials to appropriately pretest students on core ideas that are needed for upcoming instructional units, you can identify which students need help and the nature of the help they need before they fail. By then using appropriate instructional activities, you can help students acquire the core knowledge needed to be successful in the upcoming units—making that instruction effective rather than ineffective for these students.

The Research Base

Not only have these materials gone through extensive field testing with both students and teachers, the CBA approach is consistent with major scientific theories describing how students learn mathematics *with understanding*. These theories agree that mathematical ideas must be personally constructed by students as they intentionally try to make sense of situations, and that to be effective, mathematics teaching must carefully guide and support students' construction of personally meaningful mathematical ideas (Baroody and Ginsburg, 1990; Battista, 1999, 2001; Bransford, Brown, and Cocking, 1999; De Corte, Greer, and Verschaffel, 1996; Greeno, Collins, and Resnick, 1996; Hiebert and Carpenter, 1992; Lester, 1994; National Research Council, 1989; Prawat, 1999; Romberg, 1992; Schoenfeld, 1994; Steffe and Kieren, 1994; von Glasersfeld, 1995). Research shows that when students' current ideas and beliefs are ignored, their development of mathematical understanding suffers. And conversely, "There is a good deal of evidence that learning is enhanced when teachers pay attention to the knowledge and beliefs that learners bring to a learning task, use this knowledge as a starting point for new instruction, and monitor students' changing conceptions as instruction proceeds" (Bransford et al., 1999, p. 11).

The CBA approach is also consistent with research on mathematics teaching. For instance, based on their research in the Cognitively Guided Instruction program, Carpenter and Fennema (1991) concluded that teachers must "have an understanding of the general stages that students pass through in acquiring the concepts and procedures in the domain, the processes that are used to solve different problems at each stage, and the nature of the knowledge that underlies these processes" (1991, p. 11). Indeed, a number of studies have shown that when teachers learn about such research on students' mathematical thinking, they can use that knowledge in ways that positively influence their students' mathematics learning (Carpenter et al., 1998; Cobb et al., 1991; Fennema and Franke, 1992; Fennema et al., 1996; Steff and D'Ambrosio, 1995). These materials will enable you to:

- develop a detailed understanding of your students' current reasoning about specific mathematical topics, and
- choose learning goals and instructional activities to help your students build on their current ways of reasoning.

Indeed, these materials provide the kind of coherent, detailed, and well-organized research-based knowledge about students' mathematical thinking that research has indicated is important for teaching (Fennema and Franke, 1992).

Research also shows that using formative assessment can produce significant learning gains in all students (Black and Wiliam, 1998). Furthermore, formative assessment can be especially helpful for struggling students, so it can reduce achievement gaps in mathematics learning. The CBA materials offer teachers a powerful type of *formative assessment* that monitors students' learning in ways that enable teaching to be adapted to meet students' learning needs. "For assessment to function formatively, the results have to be used to adjust teaching and learning" (Black and Wiliam, 1998, p. 142). To implement high-quality formative assessment, the major question that must be asked is, "Do I really know enough about the understanding of my pupils to be able to help each of them?" (Black and Wiliam, 1998, p. 143). CBA materials help answer this question.

Using CBA Materials for RTI

Response to Intervention (RTI) is a school-based, tiered prevention and intervention model for helping all students learn mathematics. Tier 1 focuses on high-quality classroom instruction for all students. Tier 2 focuses on supplemental, differentiated instruction to address particular needs of students within the classroom context. Tier 3 focuses on intensive individualized instruction for students who are not making adequate progress in Tiers 1 and 2.

CBA can be effectively used for all three RTI tiers. For Tier 1, CBA materials provide extensive, research-based descriptions of the development of students' learning of particular mathematical topics. Research shows that teachers who understand such information about student learning teach in ways that produce greater student achievement. For Tier 2, CBA descriptions enable you to better understand and monitor each student's mathematics learning through observation, embedded assessment, questioning, informal assessment during small-group work, and formal assessment. You can then choose instructional activities that meet your students' learning needs—whole-class tasks that benefit students at all levels; different tasks for small groups of students at the same levels; and individualized supplementary student work. For Tier 3, CBA assessments and level-specific instructional suggestions provide road maps and directions for giving struggling students the long-term individualized instruction sequences they need.

Supporting Students' Development of Mathematical Reasoning

CBA materials are designed to help students move to higher levels of reasoning. It is important, however, that instruction not *demand* that students "move up" the levels with insufficient cognitive support. Such demands result in students rotely memorizing procedures that they cannot make personal sense of: *jumps in levels are made internally by students, not by teachers or the curriculum.* This does not mean that students must progress through the levels without help. Teaching helps students by providing them with the right kinds of encouragement, support, and challenges—having students work on problems that stretch, but do not overwhelm, their reasoning, asking good questions, having them discuss their ideas with other students, and sometimes showing them ideas that they don't invent themselves. But when we show students ideas, we should not demand that they use them. Instead, we should try to get students to adopt new ideas because they make personal sense of the ideas and see the new ideas as better than the ideas they currently possess.

Chapter 1

Introduction to Understanding Fractions

In elementary school, a *fraction* is a symbolic expression of the form a/b, where *a* and *b* are whole numbers and *b* is not zero (whole numbers are 0, 1, 2, 3 . . .). In junior high, fractions can be positive and negative, and later, in algebra, fractions can be more complicated expressions. Fractions describe quantities as portions or parts of wholes. They specify relationships between wholes and their parts. As numbers, fractions are numbers that are "in between" whole numbers.

It is difficult for students to move from working with whole numbers to working with fractions because a fractional quantity is described with *two* numbers, not one, and understanding a fraction requires one to explicitly comprehend a *relationship* between two quantities—the whole and its parts.

Critical Components of Understanding Fractions

There are several critical components of a genuine understanding of fractions. These components are discussed in the following sections.

Partitioning

Before students can understand fractions, they must understand partitioning. To partition a whole is to divide it into equal portions, like dividing a pizza equally among four people.

Being able to partition, however, does not mean that one understands fractions. For instance, a student might partition a pizza equally among four people but not understand how the pieces relate to the whole, saying simply that each person gets one piece.

Fractions

To understand fractions, students must be able to partition a whole into equal portions and understand how the portions are related to the whole. Students must also understand how fractional quantities are symbolized mathematically. So, in the fraction a/b, b (the denominator) denotes how many equal parts are in the whole, and a (the numerator) denotes how many equal parts are in the fractional quantity specified by a/b.

Iteration

Deeper understanding of the role of partitioning in fractions comes from understanding the complementary process of iteration. Partitioning starts with the whole and divides it into equal parts. Iteration starts with a part and repeats it to make the whole. Students take a major step toward substantive understanding of fractions when they understand the relationship between the processes of iteration and partitioning: iterating a piece to make a whole defines a partitioning of the whole; partitioning a whole into equal pieces defines an iteration that makes the whole.

To use iteration to create a fraction n/d of a shape, you find a part that when iterated d times makes the whole, and then iterate that part n times.

Understanding Unit Fractions

To see how iteration is used to understand unit fractions, consider the question: What fraction of the whole shape below is shaded?

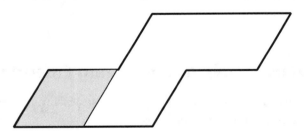

Because the shaded rhombus can be iterated 4 times to make the whole shape, the rhombus is 1/4 of the whole shape.

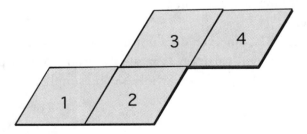

Iteration partitions the whole shape into 4 equal pieces and establishes a relationship between the shaded part and the whole—it takes 4 rhombuses to make the whole shape. Importantly, students must do more than simply iterate the rhombus; they must explicitly recognize that this iteration partitions the whole into 4 equal parts.

Understanding Non-Unit Fractions

Once students understand unit fractions, we would like them to understand non-unit, proper fractions. Again, iteration is critical. For instance, suppose we want to determine what fractional part of the whole shape below is shaded.

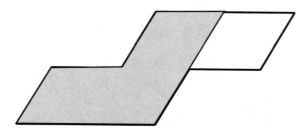

Because iterating the rhombus 4 times makes the whole shape, and iterating it 3 times makes the shaded part, the shaded part is 3/4 of the whole.

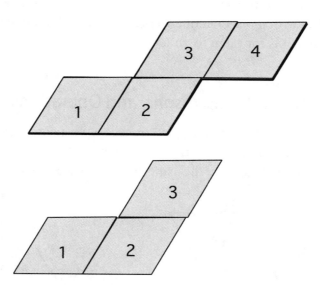

Beyond the physical iteration process, we would also like students to understand that non-unit fractions are made up of iterations of unit fractions. For instance, $3/8 = 1/8 + 1/8 + 1/8$ or $3/8 = 3 \times 1/8$.

Understanding Improper Fractions and Mixed Numerals

Students can move from using iteration to understand proper fractions to using it to understand improper fractions and mixed numerals. A *proper fraction* is a fraction in which the numerator is less than or equal to the denominator (e.g., 5/6, 3/3). An *improper fraction* is a fraction in which the numerator is greater than the denominator (e.g., 6/5). A *mixed number* has both a whole number and a fractional part (e.g., 3 4/5).

To see how iteration can be used to establish meaning for an improper fraction, consider the diagram below. Because we know that 4 iterations of the shaded rhombus makes the whole white shape, 9 iterations of the rhombus represents the improper fraction 9/4 or 2 1/4 of this whole.

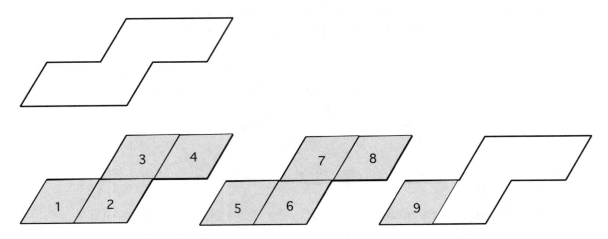

Because proper fractions deal with just one whole, and improper fractions and mixed numbers deal with more than one whole, it is easier for students to understand proper fractions than it is for them to understand improper fractions and mixed numbers.

Equivalent Fractions, Comparisons, and Operations

Another essential idea in understanding fractions is equivalent fractions. Two fractions are *equivalent* if they specify the same quantity. For example, 3/4 and 6/8 are equivalent because they specify the same amount of shading of the whole.

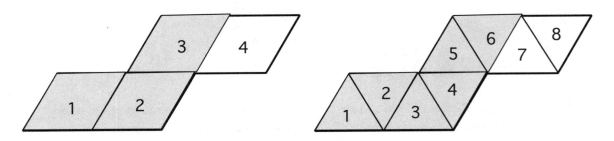

The difference in these fractions is that 3/4 specifies the quantity in terms of fourths (the rhombuses), and 6/8 specifies this same quantity in terms of eighths (the triangles). The fact that the same quantity can be named in different ways initially can be puzzling to students.

Another critical idea in dealing with fractions is that of creating fractions with common denominators. Two fractions have a *common denominator* if their denominators are equal (e.g., 2/7 and 4/7). When two fractions have a common denominator, their iterated parts are the same size, which makes it easier to compare, add, and subtract them. Consequently, to compare, add, and subtract unlike fractions (those with different denominators), we convert them to fractions with common denominators. For example, to find which is larger, 2/3 or 5/7, we convert both fractions to their equivalents using 21 as the common denominator.

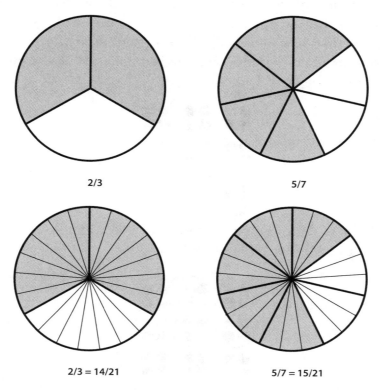

So, because 14/21 < 15/21, we know that 2/3 < 5/7.

Similarly, to add 1/4 and 1/8, we convert fourths to eighths, which gives 1/4 + 1/8 = 2/8 + 1/8 = 3/8.

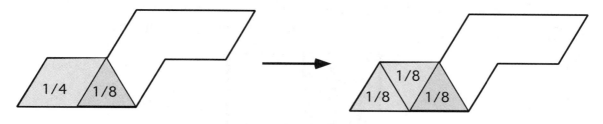

Fractions of Sets

In general, students understand fractions of whole geometric regions before they understand fractions of sets of objects or fractions of numbers. To see why, consider the problem of finding 5/9 of 36 dots.

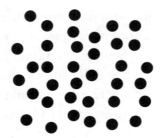

To determine one-ninth of 36, students must find a set of dots that when iterated 9 times makes 36 (i.e., they must partition 36 into 9 equivalent sets). Using objects, drawings, skip-counting, or arithmetic (36 ÷ 9 = 4), students must determine that they can iterate 4 dots 9 times to make 36. This iteration partitions 36 into 9 sets of 4 and shows that 1/9 of the set of 36 dots is 4 dots.

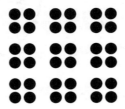

To find 5/9 of 36 dots, students must iterate a set of 4 dots 5 times. This second iteration shows that 5/9 of 36 dots is 20 dots.

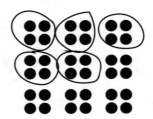

As demonstrated above, finding a fraction of a set of objects is complex because students must define and maintain a set of objects as the whole (in this case 36 dots) and then must iterate a composite unit of objects (a set of 4 dots in this case). This is considerably more difficult than, say, finding 3/4 of a square, in which the whole is one shape (the given square) and a single shape (a smaller square) must be iterated.

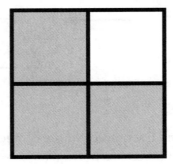

Fractions on Number Lines

Mathematicians frequently use number lines to represent and reason about numbers. Consequently, students in mathematics in and beyond algebra must often use number lines, so it is important for elementary school students to start learning about this representational tool. However, understanding number lines does not come easily for many students. To see why, let us review the steps used to represent numbers on the number line, keeping in mind that this representation is based on iterating and measuring lengths:

Step 1. Pick an arbitrary point on the line and label it zero.

Step 2. Pick another arbitrary point on the line and label it 1.

Step 3. Iterate the unit length between 0 and 1 in both directions to find the positions for all the other integers (±1, ±2, ±3,…).

Step 4. Determine the positions of fractions (rational numbers) by partitioning unit lengths into equal pieces and that can be iterated to form the whole.

Note that the choice of the point for 1 determines the positions of all other numbers, the positive direction on the number line, and the unit length (the distance between all pairs of consecutive integers is equal to the distance between 0 and 1).

A special difficulty that many students have with representing fractions on the number line arises from their lack of understanding that *numbers are represented on the number line by points, not segments*. For instance, 1/3 is represented by the point at the right end of a segment that starts at 0 and has length equal to 1/3 of the unit length.

Two-thirds is represented by the right endpoint of a segment that results from iterating a 1/3 segment twice.

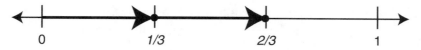

Understanding fractions as points instead of segments on a line is a big change for many students. For example, consider a student who, when asked to show 1/3 on the number line, wrote the following.

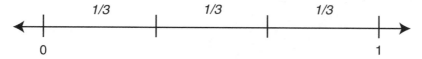

This student correctly uses her knowledge of partitioning objects to see how to divide the segment from 0 to 1 into thirds. But she sees 1/3 as a segment, not as the endpoint of a line segment starting at 0 and ending at 1/3.

Another difficulty students have with number lines arises from their lack of understanding of linear measurement. Such students count hash marks on the number line as objects in and of themselves rather than as indicators of iterations of the unit length. For example, when asked what number is represented by X on the number line below, one student counted visible hash marks and said, "There's 7 of these *[hash marks]*; X is at 3. So X is 3/7."

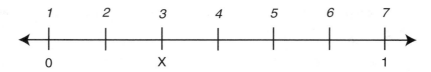

Making the Unit Explicit

Fractional amounts are always relative to a unit (or whole, or 1). Many students struggle to develop a strong conceptualization of fractions because they have difficulty establishing and maintaining the unit. To help students better understand the role of the unit in fractions, it is important to make this role *explicit* in classroom discussions. For instance, 1/2 of a pizza or rectangle is greater than 1/3 of the *same* pizza or rectangle.

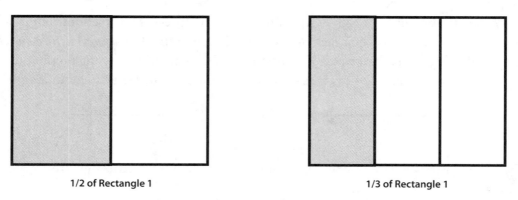

1/2 of Rectangle 1   1/3 of Rectangle 1

Similarly, 1/2 of a set of 12 dots is greater than 1/3 of the same set of 12 dots. More abstractly, if we say that 1/2 is larger than 1/3, we really mean that 1/2 of the unit or 1 is greater than 1/3 of the same unit or 1.

However, if the unit changes, then statements like "1/2 is greater than 1/3" can get complicated. For instance, as shown below, 1/2 of Rectangle 2 is smaller than 1/3 of Rectangle 3.

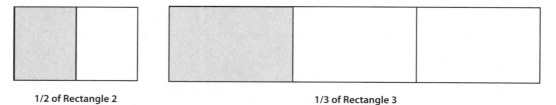

1/2 of Rectangle 2   1/3 of Rectangle 3

There is a subtle, but extremely important issue here that may underlie some fundamental student misconceptions. In many discussions by accomplished users of fractions (including many textbook explanations), when they say "one-half" without any further specification (such as one-half of something specific), the unit or 1 is implicit or "assumed understood" rather than explicit. When we are talking about pure numbers, 1/2 always equals 1/2.

However, when we are talking about 1/2 of something—like pizzas, or sets of cupcakes, or even numbers (1/2 of 10 versus 1/2 of 30)—1/2 may be unequal to 1/2 because it is 1/2 of one thing versus 1/2 of a different thing. So be careful with language. Whenever you refer to 1/2 "of something," be sure that you include the something in the reference—say, "one-half of this pizza," not "one-half."

Similarly, be explicit about what the unit is when adding or subtracting fractions. For example (continuing with the above pictures), 1/2 of Rectangle 1 + 1/3 of Rectangle 1 makes 5/6 of Rectangle 1. We keep the rectangle constant throughout the addition.

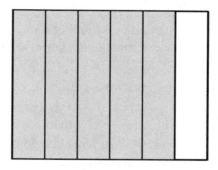

5/6 of the Rectangle

Understanding Students' Levels of Sophistication for Fractions

The CBA levels provide a detailed description of the development of students' reasoning about fractions. This detail is critical for tailoring instruction to meet students' learning needs. However, when you are first learning a set of CBA levels, the amount of detail can be overwhelming. So, keep in mind that understanding CBA levels comes in stages and develops over time. First, you will learn the major features of the levels-of-sophistication framework for fractions. As you use CBA with your students, you will learn the details of the framework.

Zooming Out to Get an Overview

To begin understanding the CBA levels for fractions, it is important to develop an understanding of the overall organization of the levels. The chart on page 10 shows the CBA fractions levels in a "zoomed out" view.

CBA Levels of Sophistication in Students' Reasoning About Fractions	
Level	**Description**
0	Student has no concept of the meaning of fractions, but may understand partitioning.
1	Student recognizes only familiar pictures of fractions.
2	Student understands fractions as counting all parts and shaded parts.
3	Student understands fractions as partitioning a whole shape into equal parts and selecting parts.
4	Student understands fractions as partitioning a quantity into equal parts and selecting some parts.
5	Student can manipulate or imagine visual representations of fractions to solve simple fraction arithmetic problems.
6	Student uses and has some intuitive understanding of symbolic fraction computation.
7	Student uses pictures or materials to solve difficult fraction arithmetic problems and to understand more precisely why fraction computations work.

These broad levels describe the major ways students reason about fractions. The levels suggest an overall learning sequence: in Levels 1–3 students develop limited conceptualizations of fractions, which in Level 4 matures into a more general and abstract conceptualization. In Levels 5–7 students develop increasingly sophisticated reasoning about arithmetic operations on fractions.

Understanding Algorithms

A computational algorithm is a precisely specified sequence of actions performed on written symbols that systematically solves one general type of computational problem.

The levels of sophistication in Cognition-Based Assessment (CBA) describe students' development of core concepts and ways of reasoning about fractions. An important part of this development is understanding and becoming fluent with using computational algorithms. *However, if algorithms are taught too early in students' development of reasoning about fractions, students cannot understand the algorithms conceptually, so they learn them by rote.* Indeed, most students in traditional instruction learn traditional algorithms for fractions rotely, without understanding the underlying number properties. Students who learn computational algorithms for fractions before achieving Level 5 reasoning will learn them rotely.

Zooming in to Meet Individual Students' Needs

Understanding individual students' reasoning precisely enough to maximize their learning or remediate a learning difficulty requires a detailed picture. We must "zoom in" to see sublevels (see Figure 1.1). The "jumps" between sublevels must be

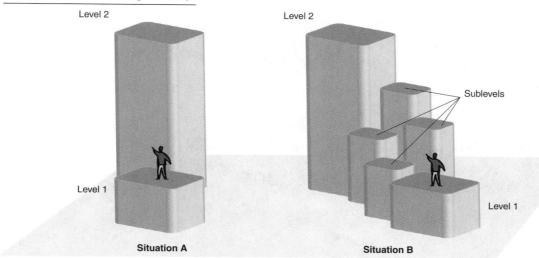

Figure 1.1 Accessible Cognitive Jumps

small enough that students can achieve them with small amounts of instruction in relatively short periods of time.

Imagine students trying to climb to a cognitive plateau needed to meet an instructional goal. In Situation A, the student has to make a cognitive jump that is too great. In Situation B, the student can get to the goal by using accessible CBA sublevels as stepping-stones. To provide students the instructional guidance and cognitive support they need to develop a thorough understanding of mathematical ideas, you need to understand and use the sublevels. Chapter 2 provides detailed descriptions and illustrations of all the CBA levels and sublevels for fractions.

CBA Levels and Preparation for Algebra

CBA levels focus on the development of concepts and reasoning, in addition to computational fluency. However, students often learn computational algorithms for fractions by rote, without understanding the underlying number properties. This rote learning not only hinders students' development of understanding of computation, it deprives them of foundational ideas needed to understand and master algebra. The CBA levels of sophistication focus on students' development of this foundational numerical reasoning. These levels trace students' development from intuitive concepts and reasoning to the number-property-based fluency with computational procedures that serves as the conceptual foundation for algebraic reasoning.

Chapter 2

Levels of Sophistication in Student Reasoning: Fractions

The CBA approach to guiding students' development of understanding of fractions builds on the CBA levels of sophistication in students' reasoning. Understanding these levels enables teachers to tailor instruction to meet students' individual learning needs. The major CBA levels (Levels 0, 1, 2, 3, 4, 5, 6, and 7) provide an overview of the ways that students think about fractions. These levels describe how students progress from beginning understanding of fraction concepts to meaningful use of fraction algorithms.

Understanding students' reasoning precisely enough to maximize their learning or remediate their learning difficulties, however, requires a more detailed picture than is provided by the major levels, so the major levels are divided into sublevels. The "jumps" between sublevels are small enough that students can achieve them with small amounts of instruction in relatively short periods of time. Sublevels serve as accessible stepping-stones in students' development.

The following chart summarizes the CBA levels for student's reasoning about fractions. The following pages provide a detailed description of each level, along with examples of student work at each level. At first glance, the amount of detail in the CBA levels can be overwhelming. So keep in mind that understanding CBA levels develops gradually as you study examples of students' work and as you use CBA with your students.

Level	Sublevel	Description	Page
0		**Student has no concept of the meaning of fractions, but may understand partitioning.**	13
	0.1	Student cannot partition objects into equal parts or subsets.	16
	0.2	Student can partition objects and sets into equal parts, but does not understand these parts as fractions.	17
1		**Student recognizes only familiar pictures of fractions.**	18
2		**Student understands fractions as counting all parts and shaded parts.**	21
3		**Student understands fractions as partitioning a whole shape into equal parts and selecting parts.**	25
4		**Student understands fractions as partitioning a quantity into equal parts and selecting some parts.**	32
	4.1	Student uses pictorial or physical materials to understand and find fractions as quantities.	36
	4.2	Student uses mental models, not physical or pictorial materials, to understand and find fractions as quantities.	40
5		**Student can manipulate or imagine visual representations of fractions to solve simple fraction arithmetic problems.**	41
6		**Student uses and has some intuitive understanding of symbolic fraction computation.**	50
7		**Student uses pictures or materials to solve difficult fraction arithmetic problems and to understand more precisely why symbolic fraction computations work.**	53

LEVEL 0: Student Has No Concept of the Meaning of Fractions, but May Understand Partitioning

Students at this level have no concept of the meaning of fractions. When they are given fraction tasks, they use whole numbers rather than fractions to describe portions of objects or sets. For example, asked how much of the rectangle below is shaded, a student at Level 0 would say 2 instead of 2/3.

Students at Level 0 differ in their understanding of partitioning, which is a critical prerequisite for fraction reasoning. There are two sublevels of reasoning about partitioning. At Level 0.1, students are unable to partition objects or sets into equal parts or subsets. At Level 0.2 students are able to partition objects or sets into equal parts, *but they do not understand these parts as fractions.* Reasoning at these two sublevels can be discriminated only by giving students partitioning tasks, not fraction tasks. It is important to note that although it is easier for students to understand partitioning of sets of objects than it is for them to understand portioning whole objects, it is easier for students to start understanding fractions by working with whole shapes.

Because students have no concept of the meaning of fractions, if they use numerical procedures for arithmetic operations, comparing fractions, or finding equivalent fractions, that use is rote.

The examples below are separated into two sections: reasoning on fraction tasks, which students at both sublevels do the same way; and reasoning on partitioning tasks, which students at the sublevels do differently.

Levels 0.1 and 0.2: Reasoning on Fraction Tasks

Students who are reasoning at the prefraction level use whole-number reasoning on fraction problems.

EXAMPLES

Task: *Tell what fraction is shaded.*

Response: 1.	**Response:** 7.

Task: *Shade 2/5 of the black box.*

Response:

Cognition-Based Assessment and Teaching of Fractions

Task:

Shade 1/4 of the circles.   *Shade 3/4 of the circles.*   *Shade 2/3 of the circles.*

Response 1:

I did 1.   This is 3 from the top number.   2 is on top.

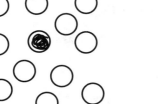   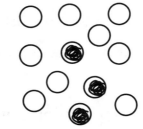   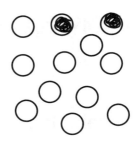

Response 2:

"1; 1, 2, 3, 4."   "1, 2, 3; 1, 2, 3, 4."   "1, 2; 1, 2, 3."

Task: *What is 5/4 of 12?*

Response: You do 5 groups of 4. That makes 20.

Task: *Find the following.*

2/3 of 9 = _____

Response: You multiply the 3 times 9.

2/3 of 9 = 27

Task: *Name the fraction marked by X on the number line.*

Response: *[Counts the first 4 hash marks]* It's 4.

Level 0.1 and 0.2: Reasoning on Partitioning Tasks

Students at Levels 0.1 and 0.2 respond differently on partitioning tasks, as shown below.

Level 0.1: Students cannot partition objects into equal parts or subsets.

Students cannot partition objects or sets of objects into equal portions or parts.

EXAMPLES

Task: *Three people want to share 6 cookies equally. How many cookies should each person get?*

Response: I could have 3 and you could have 2 and my sister could have 1. *[Teacher: Is that fair? Does everybody have the right amount?]* I like cookies. And my sister is younger than me and is small. So she only wants 1.

Task: *Three people want to share the pizza below equally. Show how much each person gets.*

Response: I divided the pizza into 3 pieces. Each person gets a piece.

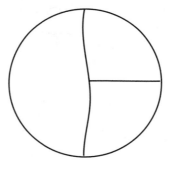

Task: *Four people want to share 5 cakes equally. Show or tell how much each person gets.*

Response: Each person gets one cake, and there's a whole cake left over for later.

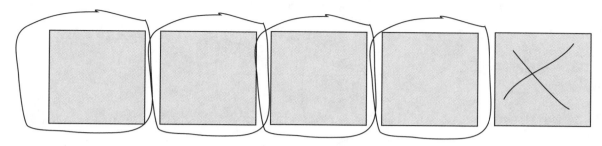

For strategies to help students at Level 0.1, see Chapter 3, page 61.

Level 0.2: Student can partition objects and sets into equal parts, but does not understand these parts as fractions.

At this level, students can partition objects and sets into equal portions, but they cannot name the fractions represented by the partitioned pieces.

EXAMPLES

Task: *Three people want to share 6 cubes equally. How many cubes should each person get?*

Response: *[Draws 3 faces, then deals cubes one at a time to the faces.]* Each person gets 2 cubes.

Task: *Four people want to share the pizza below equally. Show or tell how much each person gets.*

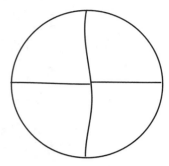

Response: *[Draws segments on the pizza as shown.]* Each person gets one piece. *[Teacher: How much of a whole pizza is each piece?]* It's one whole piece.

Task: *Four people want to share these 5 cakes equally. Show or tell how much each person gets.*

Response: *[Counts the first 4 cakes]* Each person gets one cake. *[Draws to divide the fifth cake into 4 equal pieces and counts the pieces.]* And each person gets one of these pieces of cake. So each person gets 2 pieces. *[Teacher: How many whole cakes does each person get?]* Two. *[Teacher, pointing at one of the fourths in the fifth cake: How much of a whole cake is this piece?]* It's one piece.

In the last two examples, the student was able to correctly partition the objects given to him, but he could not name the fractions represented by the partitioned parts.

For strategies to help students at Level 0.2, see Chapter 3, page 64.

LEVEL 1: Student Recognizes Only Familiar Pictures of Fractions

At this level, students associate fraction names only with standard pictures they have seen for commonly used fractions. For instance, students might associate the names one-half and one-fourth (or half, fourth) with the pictures on the next page.

But students do not understand the critical attributes of a fraction picture, such as that all subdivisions of the whole must be equal. So students might say that 1/3 of the circle below is shaded, not recognizing that the three parts are not equal. (Although elementary students cannot figure out the value of the fraction shown below, this task is still useful for determining whether they mistakenly think it is 1/3.)

At this level, students' conceptualization of fractions is restricted to specific images. For example, when asked to find 1/4 of a dozen, one third-grader said, "How can 3 be one quarter of a dozen when one quarter is just a little piece?" (Ball, 1993, p. 175). He drew the figure below.

When asked to draw a fraction, students try to recall previous images labeled as fractions rather than thinking through the fraction-creation process. Iteration and partitioning play no part in students' reasoning about fractions. As in Level 0, if students use numerical procedures for arithmetic operations, comparing fractions, or finding equivalent fractions, that use is rote.

EXAMPLES

Task: *Circle the figures below that show one-half.*

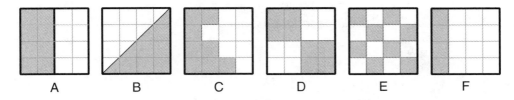

Response: Shape A looks like a half. The rest are not halves.

Task: *Circle the pictures below that show 3/4. Explain your answers.*

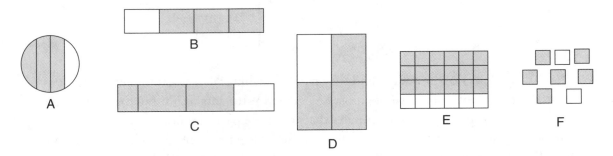

Response: I think A, B, C, and D look like 3/4. E and F don't look like 3/4.

Task: *Tell what fraction of each shape is shaded.*

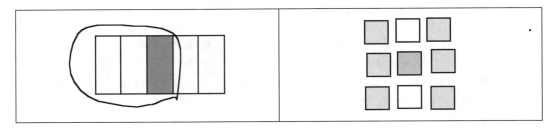

Response: This part looks like 1/3.   Looks like 7.

Task: *If this (orange) is one, what is this (red)?*

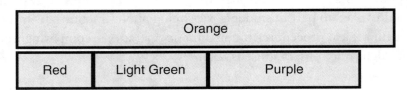

Response: *[She puts a red, light green, and purple rods next to the orange, then removes them.]* I'd say a fourth.

Task: *Tell what fraction of the large square is shaded.*

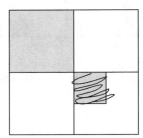

Response: *[Scribbles over the small shaded square]* It's 1/4.

This student scribbled over the part of the figure that did not fit into his standard image for 1/4.

For strategies to help students at Level 1, see Chapter 3, page 68.

LEVEL 2: Student Understands Fractions as Counting All Parts and Shaded Parts

To identify a pictorial or physical representation of a fraction, students employ the mental procedure, "count all parts, count shaded parts." Sometimes they count equal parts of a shape, sometimes unequal parts. Students don't explicitly focus on the whole. If there are not shaded and unshaded parts, students count some other visually noticeable aspect of the shapes. Neither iteration nor partitioning the whole into equal parts plays a part in students' reasoning about fractions at this level.

Students at this level don't have an explicit idea of the whole, so they have great difficulty finding fractions of sets of objects because doing so requires them to consider the set as the whole. So, when dealing with fractions of sets of objects, students use whole-number rather than fractional reasoning, such as counting just the shaded objects in a set.

Students compare fractions (less than, equal to, greater than) by drawing and inspecting pictures. However, when comparing fractions by drawing pictures, students generally are not careful to make the wholes equal. Students also have difficulty understanding improper fractions; they can't visually conceive of a fraction being more than a whole shape.

If students use numerical procedures for arithmetic operations, comparing fractions, or finding equivalent fractions, that use is rote.

EXAMPLES

Task: *Circle the figures below that show one-half.*

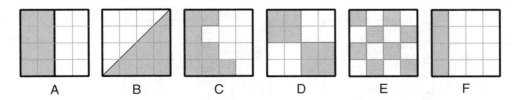

A   B   C   D   E   F

Response: A, B, C, and F are halves because one part is shaded and one part is not.

Task: *Circle the shapes below that show 3/4.*

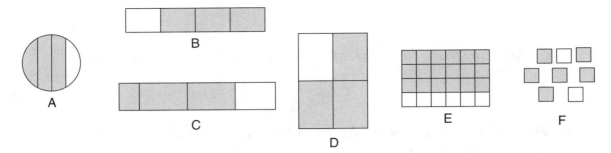

Response: A, B, C, and D are 3/4 because they all have 4 parts and 3 are shaded. E and F are not 3/4.

Task: *Tell what fraction of the large square is shaded.*

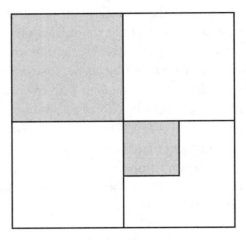

Response: *[Counts 2 shaded parts and 5 total parts]* 2/5.

Note that in several of the previous responses, students did not count equal parts.

Task: *Which fraction is larger, 2/3 or 2/5? Explain with pictures or words.*

Response: *[After drawing the figures below]* They're the same.

This student did not keep the whole constant when making fraction pictures to compare.

Task: *Shade 2/5 of the black rectangle.*

Response: You're supposed to shade 2 out of 5 parts. So here's the 5 *[drawing a vertical segment to make a column of 5]*, here's the 2 *[shading 2 of 5]*.

This student could not think of 2/5 of the whole rectangle. He needed 5 discrete but connected items to correspond to the 5 in the denominator.

Task: *Draw a picture to show 4/3. Explain your answer.*

Response:

[Teacher: What fraction did you draw?] Four-thirds. *[Teacher: Why did you draw it this way?]* The bigger number tells how many parts are in the shape; the smaller number tells how many to shade. You can't shade more parts than you have. *[Teacher: Is 4/3 larger or smaller than 1?]* It's smaller; some parts are shaded and some are not.

Because the student thinks fractions must be portions of one whole, she draws 3/4 instead of 4/3. Her conception of her fraction-drawing procedure—"You can't shade more parts than you have"—forces her to always draw proper fractions.

Task: *What is 5/4 of 20?*

Response: *[After drawing the picture below]* I drew 5 groups of 4. That's 20.

Task: *Which is bigger, 4/4 or 5/5?*

Response: This is 4/4 *[placing 4 red cubes on the table].* This is 5/5 *[placing 5 green cubes on the table].* So 5/5 is more.

Note that the unit or one is not kept constant. For the red cubes, the unit is the set of 4 cubes, but for the green cubes, the unit is the set of 5 cubes.

Task: *Name the fraction marked by X on the number line.*

Response 1: After counting and numbering all hash marks, the student says that 1 is at 6, and X is at 3, so X is 3/6.

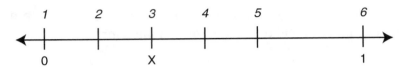

Response 2: Student counts spaces between hash marks as shown below, getting 2/5.

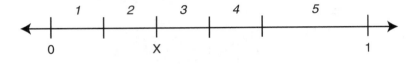

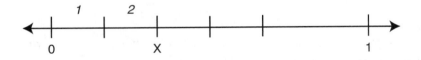

Task: *Find 1/3 + 1/5.*

Response: I drew 1/3 and 1/5, then counted the shaded parts and all the parts. It's 2/8.

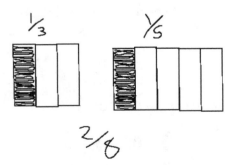

For strategies to help students at Level 2, see Chapter 3, page 68.

LEVEL 3: Student Understands Fractions as Partitioning a Whole Shape into Equal Parts and Selecting Parts

Students at this level understand fractions as being created by partitioning a whole shape into equal parts and selecting parts. Students' use of partitioning is successful, however, only when finding fractions of explicitly specified whole shapes. They have difficulty finding fractions of sets of objects, finding improper fractions, and performing arithmetic operations on shapes because in these situations the whole is more difficult to maintain. Students' reasoning is restricted to operating on shapes; they do not reason about quantities such as numbers or measurements of area.

Students use two important processes to partition a whole object into equal parts—splitting and iterating. As an example, consider students using these processes to find 3/4 of a whole shape. To find 3/4 of the rectangle, students might split the rectangle in half vertically and horizontally to divide the rectangle into 4 equal parts, then shade 3 parts.

Given pattern blocks, to find 3/4 of the whole shape below, students can iterate the rhombus block 4 times to make the whole shape, then iterate it 3 times to make 3/4 of the shape.

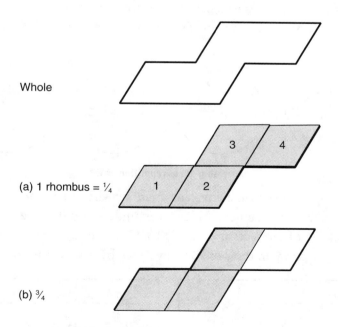

Other Characteristics and Illustrations of Level 3 Reasoning

- Students understand how to use partitioning to create unit fractions (like 1/4) before non-unit fractions (like 3/4).

- Students recognize that the equal parts in a fraction partition don't have to be congruent if the parts can be rearranged to look the same. (See example below.)

- Students compare fractions to determine if one is less than, equal to, greater than by drawing and inspecting pictures, being careful to make both the wholes equal and the parts within wholes equal.

- Students often lose track of the whole when operating on fractions. For instance, in the problem below, students who are reasoning at Level 3 see that the pieces are not equal, but they do not recognize that Harry also loses track of the unit or whole—his use of 5 as the denominator implies that he is using 5 parts (the two bars together) as the whole.

Task: *Asked to find 1/2 + 1/3, Harry drew the picture at the right and said, "1 of 2 parts, plus 1 of 3 parts = 2 of 5 parts." Tell whether Harry's reasoning is correct or incorrect and explain why.*

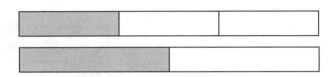

- Students do not fully understand improper fractions, although they are beginning to develop some understanding via the process of visually iterating a unit fraction. For example, a student might think of 4/3 as visually iterating a picture of 1/3 four times (see below). But the student does not explicitly see the relation between 4/3 and the original whole (so does not really understand that 4/3 is 1 1/3).

Expressing 4/3 as repetition of 1/3

- Students might recognize equivalent fractions when their equivalence is demonstrated visually. For instance, students can understand that the picture below shows that 5/6 of the rectangle equals 10/12 of the rectangle. However, students are unable to show, on their own, equivalence by drawing appropriate partitions.

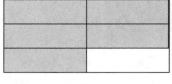

5/6

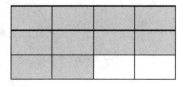

10/12

⊞ Because students have difficulty keeping track of the whole, they usually cannot perform arithmetic operations on fractions in meaningful and correct ways. For instance, in a student's picture below for 1/2 + 1/3, he recognized that the sum of 1/2 and 1/3 is not 2/3 because the parts are not equal. But he couldn't figure out how to determine a fractional expression for the sum.

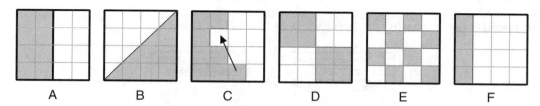

1/2

1/3

1/2 + 1/3 = ?

EXAMPLES

....

Task: *Circle the figures below that show one-half.*

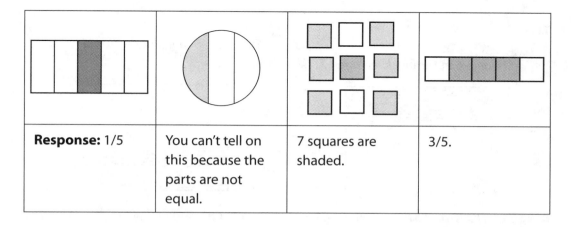

A   B   C   D   E   F

Response: A is one-half because there are 2 equal pieces and 1 is shaded. Same thing for B. On C, you just move this part here to here so the gray and white parts are the same. On D, move the bottom shaded square under the top shaded square. On E, you can move each of the shaded squares to the left to make one half. F is not one half because the gray and white parts aren't equal.

....

Task: *Tell what fraction of each shape is shaded.*

Response: 1/5	You can't tell on this because the parts are not equal.	7 squares are shaded.	3/5.

Task: *Circle the shapes below that show 3/4.*

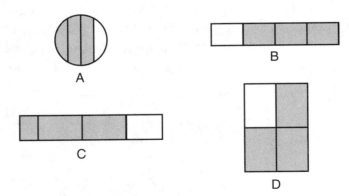

A

B

C

D

Response: Only B and D because they both have 4 equal parts and 3 shaded. The parts aren't equal in A and C.

Task: *Which fraction is larger, 2/3 or 2/5? Explain with pictures or words.*

Response: *[After drawing pictures for 2/3 and 2/5]* 2/3 is bigger.

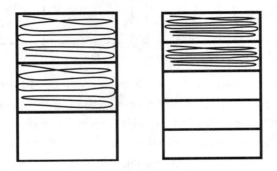

The student's representation has equal parts within fractions and equal wholes for both fractions.

Task:

Shade 2/5 of the black rectangle.

Shade 2/5 of the black rectangle in a different way.

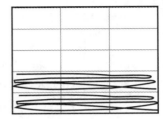

Response: *[Describing the first picture]* Each row is one fifth and we need two of them.

This student uses the grid lines to partition the rectangle into 5 equal rows.

Cognition-Based Assessment and Teaching of Fractions

Task: *Find 2/3 of the blue rod.*

Response: I think 3 light greens make the blue. *[Puts 3 light greens end-to-end under the blue]* Yep.

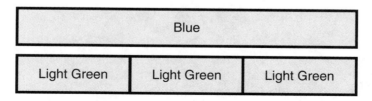

So 2/3 of the blue is two light greens *[takes one light green away]*.

This student explicitly uses iteration to find 2/3.

Task:

Shade 1/4 of the circles.   *Shade 2/3 of the circles.*

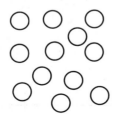   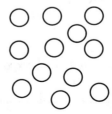

Response 1:

I did 1 out of 4.   I did 2 out of 3.

   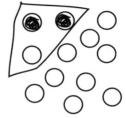

Response 2: *[for 2/3 of the circles]* I kept doing two-thirds. *[Note that although it is doubtful that the student really understands what she is doing, her answer is correct.]*

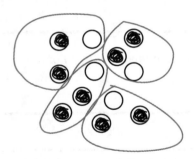

Task: *Name the fraction marked by X on the number line.*

Response: There's 5 of these equal lines *[horizontal segments]* in 1; there's 3 of these lines in X. So X is 3/5.

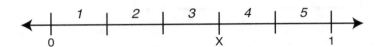

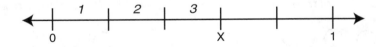

Task: *Name the fraction marked by X on the number line.*

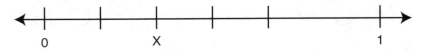

Cognition-Based Assessment and Teaching of Fractions

Response: You have to make all these spaces the same size first *[adds hash mark to last segment on the right]*. There's 6 in the whole segment; there's 2 of these in X. So X is 2/6.

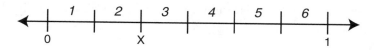

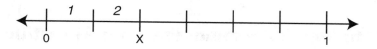

Task: *If the blue rod is one, how much is each light green rod?*

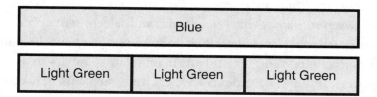

Response: Each light green is one-third.

Teacher: *How much is this?*

Response: Two-thirds.

Teacher: *How much is this?*

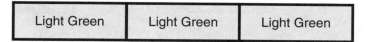

Response: Three-thirds.

Teacher: *How much is this?*

Response: Four-fourths. *[Teacher: How do you know?]* Because it takes 4 of them to make the whole light green row.

Typical of students in Level 3, this student was unable to reason validly about improper fractions.

For strategies to help students at Level 3, see Chapter 3, page 73.

LEVEL 4: Student Understands Fractions As Partitioning a Quantity into Equal Parts and Selecting Some Parts

In many ways, Level 4 is where students develop their first substantive understanding of fractions *as numbers*. Students at this level understand fractions as being created by partitioning *a numerical quantity* into equal parts and selecting or accumulating parts. When students iterate or split objects, they do so to reason about the numerical quantities the objects represent. Or students manipulate numbers to determine how to partition objects. In Level 4, students have created a new link between number and shape that enables them to flexibly go back and forth between actions on objects and actions on numbers, and to generalize their fraction understanding to multiple contexts (including sets).

For instance, in Level 3, because students reason about shapes, the top row of the figure below convinces students that the shaded section on the right is 3/4. But in Level 4, because students reason about quantity (in this case area), given the top row, students also can consider different shapes as representing 1 and 3/4, as shown in the bottom row.

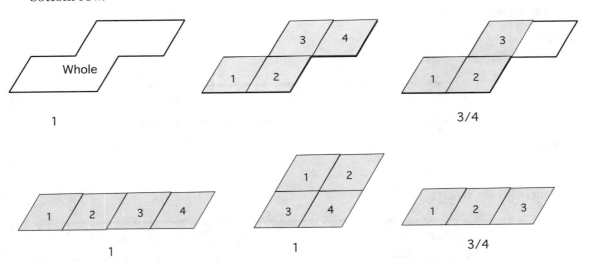

Because of students' more abstract understanding of fractions, they more explicitly understand the whole, the part, and the fraction creation process. This enables them to keep track of and maintain the whole—so they can find fractions of sets of objects and find improper fractions.

Other Characteristics and Illustrations of Level 4 Reasoning

▦ Because students focus on quantity instead of shape, they understand that, for a fraction, equal subdivisions of the whole can be judged *numerically*. For example, a student can conclude that half the large square below is shaded because he determines that 8 of the small squares are shaded and 8 are not shaded.

▦ Students can properly conceptualize fractions of sets of objects. For example, suppose students are asked to shade 2/3 of the circles in the picture below.

Students see that the whole is 12 circles, that there are 3 equal sets of 4 circles in the whole, so, after looping the 3 sets, they shade the circles in 2 of these sets and see that 8 circles is 2/3 of the set of 12 circles.

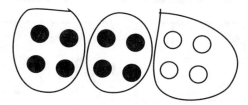

▦ Because of students' more explicit understanding of the whole in the fraction creation process, they can use visual representations to create improper fractions (e.g., 4/3) and understand the relationship between improper fractions and mixed numerals (e.g., 4/3 = 1 1/3). For instance, asked to show 4/3, students draw a figure like that below and can use the figure to explain why 4/3 equals 1 1/3.

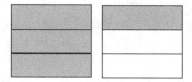

⊞ Students can use *given* pictures to establish that two fractions are equivalent. For instance, given a picture of 5/6 and asked to show that 5/6 is equivalent to 10/12, students subdivide each sixth into 2 equal pieces to show the equivalence.

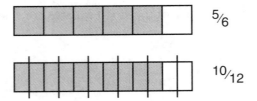

Or, asked to use the 6-by-4 rectangle below to show that 10/12 is equivalent to 5/6, students create two partitions of the shaded area to show the equivalence. (See the rectangles in the bottom row below.)

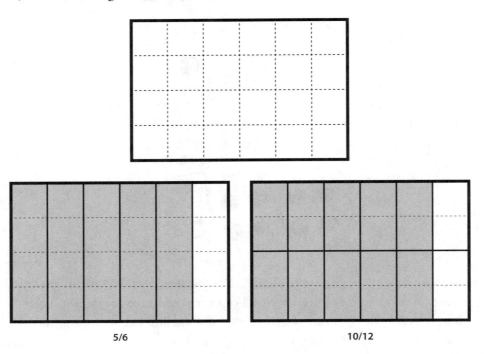

⊞ Students can compare fractions to determine if one is less than, equal to, or greater than another by drawing shapes, then comparing area measurements of shape partitions. For instance, students might reason that 1/2 is greater than 1/3 in the picture below because 1/2 is 12 one-by-one squares and 1/3 is 8 squares. They understand that the whole, 1, is 24 squares. In this case, students are attending to the areas of fraction regions. However, they may not be thinking explicitly "this is the area of this region"; it is an implicit focus on area units (squares).

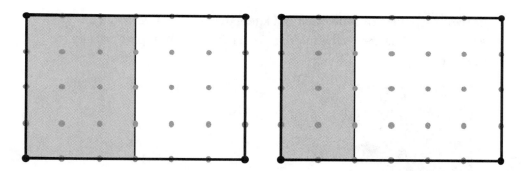

■ Not only can students perform the fraction-creation process, they can understand the meaning of actions taken in the process and alter the sequence of actions if necessary. This enables students to reverse the sequence of actions in the fraction-creation process so that they can construct the whole from a fractional part. For instance, students can solve problems like the one below:

The picture below shows 2/3. Find the whole.

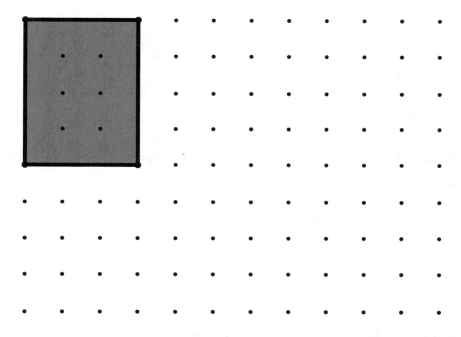

Response: *[Draws as shown below]* I knew that 2/3 has two equal parts, so I drew this line across the middle. Then I drew another part just like the first two.

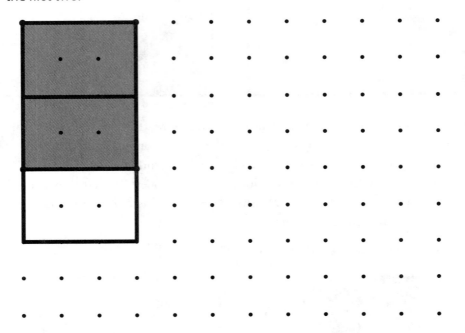

Note: Students don't acquire all this reasoning at the same time. It evolves gradually with appropriate experiences.

Level 4.1: Student uses pictorial or physical materials to understand and find fractions as quantities.

Students use pictorial or physical materials to understand fractions as being created by partitioning *a numerical quantity* into equal parts and selecting or accumulating parts.

EXAMPLES

Task: *Circle the figures below that show one-half.*

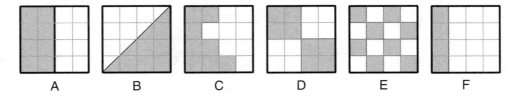

Response: A, B, C, D, and E are each one-half because 8 squares are shaded and 8 are not shaded.

Task: *Tell what fraction of each shape is shaded.*

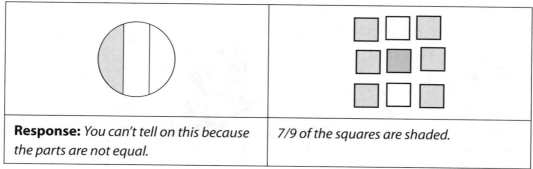

| **Response:** *You can't tell on this because the parts are not equal.* | *7/9 of the squares are shaded.* |

Task: *Mary says that 3/4 of the shape is shaded. Is Mary right or wrong? Explain your answer.*

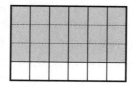

Response: There are 4 equal rows, so each row is 1/4, and 3 rows is 3/4.

Task: *Which fraction is larger, 8/9 or 6/7? Explain with pictures or words.*

Response: *[After drawing a picture]* They both have 1 piece missing. But the piece missing in 8/9 is smaller than the piece in 6/7, so 8/9 is bigger.

Task:

Shade 2/5 of the black rectangle.

Shade 2/5 of the black rectangle in a different way.

Response: *[First picture]* A row is one-fifth and there's 3 little rectangles in a row. So you just need to shade any 6 little rectangles.

Task: *For each problem, a fractional part of a whole cake is shaded. Show the whole cake.*

Response: *[For 1/4]* It's a fourth, so you make 4 equal parts for the whole.

[For 3/4] I made the 3 in the shaded part because this is *three*-fourths. I made another fourth so there are 4 for the whole.

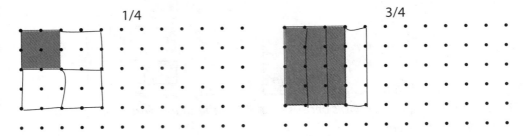

Three steps are necessary to make fraction pictures: (1) Represent the whole. (2) Divide the whole into the denominator number of equal parts. (3) Select the numerator number of the equal parts. To be successful on problems in which students are given a fraction and must find the whole, students must have abstracted this fraction-creation sequence sufficiently to reverse it. The above student could conceptualize each given shaded part as the result of steps 1–3, and he could reverse the sequence of steps. For instance, he could see that the shaded part for 3/4 was the result of dividing the whole into 4 equal parts, then iterating (selecting) 3 of these parts. To reverse this sequence, he had to divide the given shaded area into 3 parts, then make four copies of one of these parts.

Task: *Find 2/3 of 9.*

Response: *[Draws the picture]* 6.

Task: *What is 5/4 of 20?*

Response: *[After drawing the picture below]* Twenty dots is the whole. Divide it into fourths; 5 dots is a fourth. So 5 groups of 5 dots is 5/4 of 20. So it's 25.

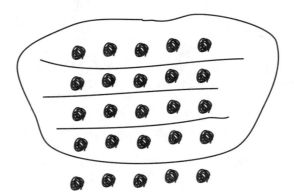

Task: *The 6 cookies below are 3/4 of a bag of cookies. How many cookies were in the whole bag?*

Response: *[After looping groups of 2 in the picture below]* When I find 3/4, I find the fourths, then take 3 of them. The 6 cookies are 3 of the fourths. So divide the 6 into 3 groups to get fourths—the whole bag is 8 cookies.

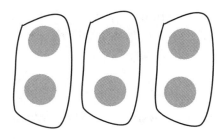

Task: *Asked to find 1/2 + 1/3, Harry drew the picture at the right and said, "1 of 2 parts, plus 1 of 3 parts equals 2 of 5 parts. So it's 2/5."*
Tell whether Harry's reasoning is correct or incorrect and explain why.

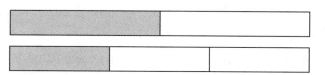

Response: Harry is wrong because he does not have equal pieces and he uses two wholes when counting pieces.

Task: *If this [4 light green rods] is 2/3, show 1.*

Light Green	Light Green	Light Green	Light Green

Response: Two of these [dark greens] makes this [the 4 light greens].

Light Green	Light Green	Light Green	Light Green
Dark Green		Dark Green	

So you need 3 of these [dark greens] to make 1.

Dark Green	Dark Green	Dark Green

For strategies to help students at Level 4.1, see Chapter 3, page 82.

Level 4.2: Student uses mental models, not physical or pictorial materials, to understand and find fractions as quantities.

For fractions involving small numbers, students use mental models, not pictorial or physical materials, to understand fractions as created by partitioning *a numerical quantity* into equal parts and selecting or accumulating parts. Students have abstracted their previous manipulations of physical and pictorial material into mental models that enable them to act on numbers rather than visual material.

EXAMPLES

....

Task: *Mary says that 3/4 of the shape is shaded. Is Mary right or wrong? Explain your answer.*

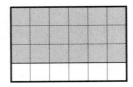

Response: She's right; the picture shows 18/24, which equals 3/4 because you can divide 18 into 3 groups of 6 and 24 into 4 groups of 6.

Although the student had to inspect the picture to understand the problem, she used numerical reasoning to determine that 18/24 is 3/4.

....

Task: *Which fraction is larger, 2/3 or 2/5? Explain with pictures or words.*

Response 1: 2/3 is bigger because the top numbers are the same, and thirds are bigger than fifths.

Response 2: 2/3 is bigger because 2/3 is bigger than 1/2 and 2/5 is smaller than 1/2.

....

Task: *Which fraction is larger, 8/9 or 6/7? Explain with pictures or words.*

Response: The piece missing in 8/9 is smaller than the piece in 6/7, so 8/9 is bigger.

....

Task: *What is 3/4 of 36?*

Response: 36 divided into 4 equal groups gives 9 in each group. And I need 3 groups; 27.

....

Task: *What is 5/4 of 20?*

Response: To find 1/4 of 20, divide 20 into 4 equal groups, which is 5 in each group. So 5 fourths of 20 is 5 groups of 5, equals 25.

Task: *Six cookies are 3/4 of a bag of cookies. How many cookies are in the whole bag?*

Response: When I find 3/4 of a number, I divide the number into fourths, then find how much is in 3 of them. 6 is 3 groups of 2, so 2 is 1/4. So take four 2s makes 8.

For strategies to help students at Level 4.2, see Chapter 3, page 84.

LEVEL 5: Student Can Manipulate or Imagine Visual Representations of Fractions to Solve Simple Fraction Arithmetic Problems

Students' understanding of the meaning of fractions is sufficient that they can manipulate visual representations of fractions to solve simple fraction arithmetic problems. Problems are "simple" if they are reasonably easy to solve using pictorial/concrete reasoning or imagery-based mental computation. For instance, the problem $4 \frac{1}{2} \div \frac{1}{2}$ is simple because students can easily imagine or draw 4 pies cut into halves and one more half pie to "see" that there are 9 halves in $4 \frac{1}{2}$ whole pies. Or students might imagine $4 \frac{1}{2}$ as a quantity, without tying it to a particular physical representation such as pies, and see that there are 2 halves in each whole, so $4 \frac{1}{2}$ is 9 halves. (Simple addition and subtraction problems involve fractions with small numerators and denominators.)

As another example of this kind of reasoning, students can understand the relationship between 3/4 and 1/4 in terms of multiplication; 3/4 equals 3 times 1/4. They can use this reasoning to find, for example, 3/4 of 12 by thinking that 1/4 of 12 is 3, so 3/4 of 12 is 3 times 3, equaling 9.

As always, implementing this type of reasoning using mental imagery is more sophisticated than using actual materials or pictures.

Comparing Fractions

Students use pictures to generate families of equivalent fractions and to compare fractions by converting them to fractions with common denominators. For instance, students can draw the following to find a set of fractions equivalent to 1/2: 1/2 = 2/4 = 3/6 = 6/12.

Or, students can subdivide the 4-by-6 rectangle below in different ways to show that 5/6 is greater than 3/4 by converting these fractions to equivalent fractions with the same denominator. That is, students pictorially implement the procedure of comparing fractions by converting them to fractions with common denominators.

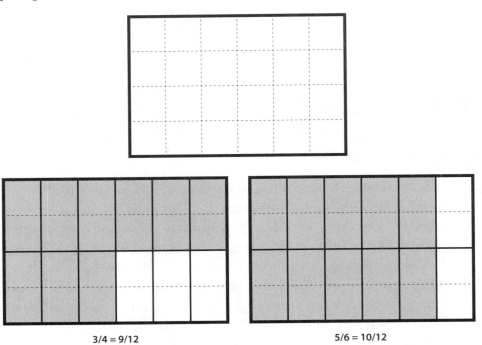

3/4 = 9/12   5/6 = 10/12

Addition and Subtraction

At this level of reasoning, students can use pictures and even imagine adding and subtracting fractions with like denominators. For instance, they understand that 1/7 plus 3/7 equals 4/7 or that 3/7 minus 1/7 is 2/7. However, for adding or subtracting fractions with unlike denominators, they need pictorial or physical representations that contain some guidance on choosing an appropriate representation for the unit or 1. For instance, to add or subtract two fractions with unlike denominators on graph paper, the problems should give students an appropriate representation of 1, such as a strip containing the number of squares in the product of the two fractions' denominators. As shown on the next page, the representation chosen for 1 to pictorially represent 1/3 + 1/5 has 3 × 5 squares in it; 15 is a common denominator for these two fractions.

Use the graph paper below to find 1/3 + 1/5. The representation for 1 is shown.

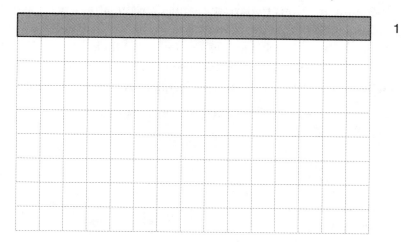

1

A student at this level might reason as follows: The 1 has 15 squares, so each square is a fifteenth. *[Drawing the second row below]* Divide 1 into 3 equal pieces, so 1/3 is 5/15. *[Drawing the third row]* Divide 1 into 5 equal pieces, so 1/5 is 3/15. *[Drawing the fourth and fifth rows]* So 1/3 + 1/5 equals 5/15 + 3/15, which is 8/15.

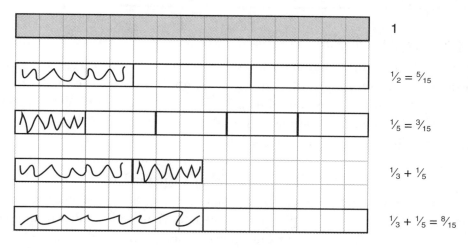

1

$\frac{1}{2} = \frac{5}{15}$

$\frac{1}{5} = \frac{3}{15}$

$\frac{1}{3} + \frac{1}{5}$

$\frac{1}{3} + \frac{1}{5} = \frac{8}{15}$

A student might use similar reasoning and a similar representation to find 1/3 – 1/5: To subtract, I need the fractions to have the same denominator. I see that 1 has 15 squares, so each square is a fifteenth. *[Drawing the second row below]* If I divide 1 into 3 equal pieces, I get 1/3 is 5/15. *[Drawing the third row]* If I divide 1 into 5 equal pieces, I see that 1/5 is 3/15. *[Drawing 1/3 again and crossing out 3/15 on it]* So the picture shows that 1/3 – 1/5 equals 2 squares, and each square is a fifteenth; so it's 2/15.

$$1$$
$$\frac{1}{3} = \frac{5}{15}$$
$$\frac{1}{5} = \frac{3}{15}$$
$$\frac{1}{3} - \frac{1}{5}$$
$$\frac{1}{3} - \frac{1}{5} = \frac{2}{15}$$

Multiplication and Division

Students working at this level often conceptualize multiplication in terms of groups or portions of some set or quantity. For whole numbers, students can think of 3×4 as 3 *groups of* 4. Similarly, they can think of $3 \times 2\ 1/2$ as 3 groups of 2 1/2, which they envision mentally or with pictures as 3 groups of 2, which is 6, and 3 groups of 1/2, which is 1 1/2. So the total is 6 + 1 1/2 = 7 1/2.

When the first factor is a fraction and the second is a whole number, students can think in terms of fractions of sets. For example, they can think of $3/4 \times 24$ as 3/4 *of* 24. To find 3/4 *of* 24, separate 24 objects into 4 equal groups (there are 6 in each); find the total in 3 groups, which is 3 groups of 6, or 18 (students might do this reasoning with physical materials, pictures, or mental imagery). Although students might use division and multiplication in solving this problem, they do so after explicitly thinking about partitioning 24 into 4 groups and selecting 3 of these groups.

Students use two kinds of physical reasoning about division problems. *Measurement reasoning* asks how many copies of the divisor are in the dividend. For instance, students might reason about 2 1/2 ÷ 1/4 by trying to determine how many fourths are in 2 1/2.

Student: [Drawing] *This is 2 1/2.*

Student: *Divide it up into fourths. There are 10 fourths in 2 1/2.*

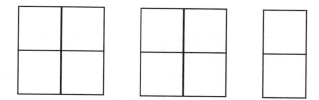

Partitive reasoning asks if the dividend is partitioned (divided) into the number of equal parts in the divisor, how much is in each part. For instance, a student might solve the problem 4 1/2 ÷ 2 by dividing 4 1/2 into 2 equal parts by drawing one of the pictures below. In the first picture, the student draws 4 1/2, circles half of 4 (2) and half of 1/2 (1/4), and gets 2 1/4.

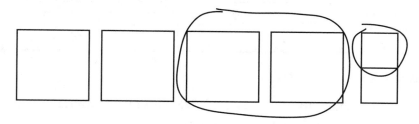

In the second picture, the student draws 4 1/2, divides each part in half, circles two halves, two halves, and 1/4, and gets 2 1/4.

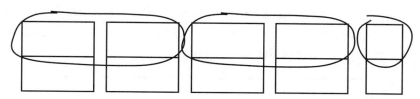

EXAMPLES

....

Task: *Use the picture below to find 1/2 + 1/5.*

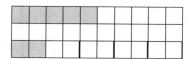

Response 1: Add the 1/5 to the 1/2.

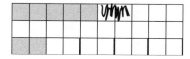

Because there are 10 squares across in the whole, it's 7/10.

Task: *Find 1/2 + 1/5.*

Response 2: Make 1/2 and 1/5.

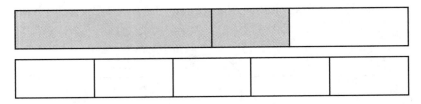

Add the 1/5 to the 1/2.

It looks like you get about 3 1/2 fifths.

Students at Level 5 can do the problem 1/2 + 1/5 with the appropriate grid (Response 1), but not without the grid (Response 2).

Task: *Find 1/4 × 1/2.*

Response: *[Shades half a rectangle horizontally.]* You need to take 1/4 of 1/2—so divide the 1/2 into 4 equal pieces and shade one piece. I'd say this is 1/8 because there are 4 pieces on the bottom, so there would be 4 on top.

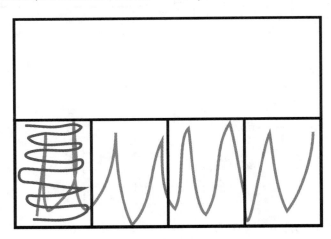

Task: *Find 1/2 ÷ 1/3.*

Response: First you make 1/2 and 1/3. You want to find out how many 1/3s are in 1/2. You can see there's one 1/3 in 1/2 but not two. So the answer is between 1 and 2.

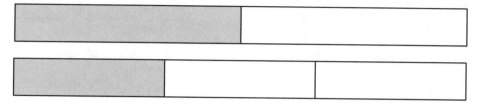

Task: *Find 1/4 + 1/2.*

Response: I know 1/2 is 2/4. *[Drawing the picture below]* Make 1/4 and 2/4. It equals 3/4.

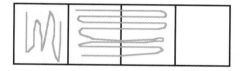

Task: *Find 2/3 × 1/2.*

Response: *[Draws picture]* I made 1/2 going this way *[horizontally]*. Then I made 2/3 going this way *[vertically]*. I saw that there were 2 squares that were shaded both ways. And the whole was divided into 6 of these squares. So my answer is 2/6.

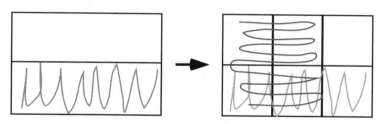

At Level 5, students make sense of this procedure. At earlier levels, if they perform it, they do so rotely. Note, however, that students generally do not discover this idea on their own—it is a result of instruction.

Task: *Find 1/2 – 1/3. [Given 1 partitioned into 6 equal pieces.]*

Response: First you make 1/2 and 1/3.

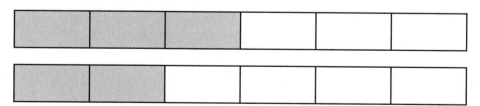

Then you make 1/2 and 1/3 into sixths, so the pieces are the same size.

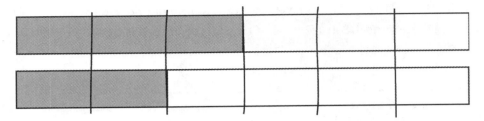

Then you take away 1/3 from 1/2.

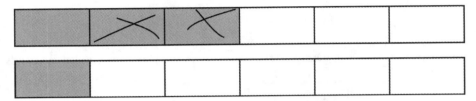

So there's 1/6 left.

Task: *Which fraction is larger, 2/3 or 2/5? Explain with pictures or words.*

Response: *[Using graph paper and making 15 squares the unit]* I need a common denominator. 2/3 equals 10/15 and 2/5 equals 6/15. So 2/3 is bigger.

Task: *Shade 2/5 of the black rectangle.*

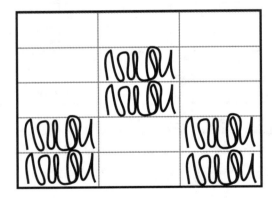

Response: There's 15 little rectangles. 1/5 of 15 is 3; so 2/5 is 6. So I can shade any 6 of the little rectangles.

Task: *Tell what fraction of the large square is shaded.*

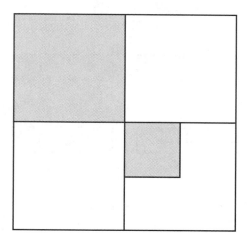

Response: The big shaded square is 1/4. The small shaded square is 1/4 of 1/4, which is 1/16 of the big square. Because the big shaded square is also 4/16, the shaded part is 4/16 plus 1/16, which is 5/16.

Task: *Show how to find 1/3 + 1/2 on the number line.*

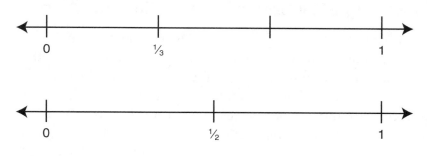

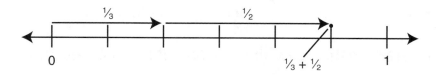

Response: *[After drawing 1/3 and 1/2]* You have to put 1/2 at the end of 1/3. But I can't find where 1/2 ends unless I get a common denominator, which is sixths. *[After drawing another number line with sixths marked, she first draws 1/3 (which is 2/6) then 1/2 (which is 3/6) to the right of 1/3.]* So 1/3 + 1/2 is 5/6.

Task: *Find 3 1/2 ÷ 1/4. [Hint. Use graph paper and make 1 equal 4 squares.]*

Response 1: I know that there are 4 fourths in 1, so 3 makes 12 fourths, and 1/2 is 2 more, so that's 14.

Response 2: *[Using the picture, counts the number of fourths in the shaded portion representing 3 1/2.]* There are 4 fourths in each whole, and 2 fourths in 1/2, that's 14.

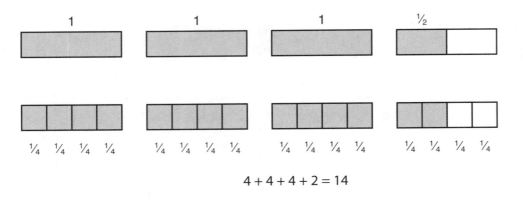

$$4 + 4 + 4 + 2 = 14$$

For strategies to help students at Level 5, see Chapter 3, page 89.

LEVEL 6: Student Uses and Has Some Intuitive Understanding of Symbolic Fraction Computation

Students can symbolically add, subtract, multiply, and divide fractions. They can also symbolically find fractions of numbers, compare fractions, and find equivalent fractions. Students can demonstrate some intuitive understanding of symbolic computations using pictorial or concrete representations, or mental imagery, on simple problems. For instance, asked why they use a common denominator when adding, subtracting, or comparing fractions, students say that they need to make the pieces equal sizes (and students can illustrate this idea with a picture for a specific pair of fractions). However, students do not understand how multiplying the numerator and denominator of a fraction by, say, 5 corresponds to subdividing the fraction pieces of the original fraction into 5 pieces—that comes only in Level 7.

Other Characteristics and Illustrations of Level 6 Reasoning

Students can use multiplication and division to find fractions of whole numbers. For example, to find 3/4 of 256, students divide 256 by 4, getting 64, then multiply the quotient 64 by 3. Asked to explain why they use this procedure, students say that you have to divide 256 into 4 equal groups, and find out how much is in 3 groups. This type of reasoning is restricted to situations in which the denominator of the fraction evenly divides the given whole number. For instance, in the above problem, 4 evenly divides 256.

Students can use multiplication and division to find equivalent fractions. For example, 10/12 is equivalent to 5/6 because both the numerator and denominator of 10/12 can be divided by 2 to get 5/6. Also, 10/12 is equivalent to 70/84 because both the numerator and denominator of 10/12 can be multiplied by 7 to get 70/84. Asked to justify that 2/3 = 10/15, students draw a picture like the one below.

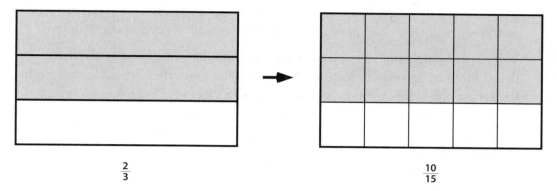

$$\frac{2}{3} \qquad\qquad\qquad \frac{10}{15}$$

Students can use multiplication and division and common denominators to compare fractions. For example, to compare 2/5 and 3/7, students convert the fractions to a common denominator of 35: 2/5 = 14/35, 3/7 = 15/35; so 3/7 > 2/5.

Students can *numerically* convert improper fractions to mixed numbers and vice versa (as opposed to pictorially in earlier levels). For example, to convert 3 4/7 to an improper fraction, students multiply 3 by 7 to determine that there are 21 sevenths in 3 wholes, then they add 4 sevenths to this to get a total of 25/7. Asked why this procedure works, the student says that there are 7 sevenths in each whole, so 21 in 3, plus 4 more makes 25. To convert 25/7 back into a mixed number, students divide 25 by 7, getting 3 with a remainder of 4, so 25/7 equals 3 and 4/7; 25 ÷ 7 = 3 means there are 3 wholes in 25 with 4 left over. Students can also justify their answers for this example using pictures or concrete materials.

In situations in which the numerator and denominator are small and the denominator divides 10 or 100, students can convert fractions to decimal fractions. For instance, students convert 3/4 into an equivalent fraction with 100 as the denominator by multiplying the numerator and denominator of 3/4 by 25 to get 3/4 = 75/100. Students can then write the fraction 75/100 in decimal notation: 75/100 = .75. Students can justify their conversions by drawing fraction partitions on a 10 by 10 grid (for example, they draw 3/4 on a 10 by 10 grid and see that 75 squares are shaded). Students can convert fractions to decimal notation by using a calculator to divide the numerator by the denominator (but they do not understand that this conversion is often an approximation, not an equivalence).

Note 1. Level 5 reasoning is a prerequisite for making personal and meaningful sense of the symbolic algorithms for fraction arithmetic. Students who learn to perform these algorithms before reaching Level 5 will learn the algorithms by rote.

Note 2. Although students at Level 6 can draw pictures to illustrate how to solve simple arithmetic problems with fractions, for difficult problems, using pictures is too complex and cumbersome. For instance, drawing a picture to show that 2 1/2 ÷ 1/4 = 10 is easy, whereas drawing a picture to show that 2 1/2 ÷ 1/3 = 7 1/2 is much more difficult and occurs in Level 7. Thus, when asked, each of the students below can use pictures to explain how to solve simple problems with arithmetic operations involving fractions (but not the difficult problems shown below). Generally, students don't volunteer this information. So the only way to know if students are performing the computational algorithms for fractions rotely or meaningfully is to ask appropriate questions as is illustrated in the examples.

Note 3. Although students at Level 6 can, and should, be exposed to algebraic descriptions of procedures for computing with fractions, they are not comfortable with these algebraic expressions. They are much more comfortable with verbal descriptions of these procedures, and with doing examples with actual numbers.

EXAMPLES

Task: *Find* $\dfrac{2}{31}+\dfrac{4}{5}$.

Response: *[Writes]*

$$2\times 5 = 10. \quad 31\times 5 = 155. \quad \dfrac{10}{155}$$

$$4\times 31 = 124. \quad 5\times 31 = 155. \quad \dfrac{124}{155}$$

$$\dfrac{10}{155}+\dfrac{124}{155}=\dfrac{134}{155}$$

You have to multiply the top and bottom of 2/31 by 5. You have to multiply the top and bottom of 4/5 by 31. Then add the new fractions.

[Teacher: Why did you do it this way?] I had to get a common denominator. *[Teacher: Why do you need a common denominator?]* So the pieces for each fraction are the same size. *[Teacher: How do you know you got equivalent fractions?]* Because in each fraction, I multiplied the top and bottom by the same number.

Task: *Find* $\dfrac{12}{13}\times\dfrac{4}{5}$.

Response: *[Writes]* $\dfrac{12}{13}\times\dfrac{4}{5}=\dfrac{12\times 4}{13\times 5}=\dfrac{48}{65}$.

[Teacher: Why did you multiply the numerators and denominators?] When we drew rectangles to multiply fractions, there was a pattern. You get the answer by multiplying the numerators and putting that on top of multiplying the denominators.

Task: *Find* $\dfrac{3}{4}\div\dfrac{2}{7}$.

Response: *[Writes]* $\dfrac{3}{4}\div\dfrac{2}{7}=\dfrac{3}{4}\times\dfrac{7}{2}=\dfrac{21}{8}=2\dfrac{5}{8}$.

[Teacher: Why did you invert and multiply?] When we drew pictures to divide fractions, there was a pattern. You get the answer by turning the second fraction upside down, then multiplying the fractions.

Task: *Find 2 1/3 × 3/5.*

Response: *[Writes]* 2 1/3 × 3/5 = 7/3 × 3/5 = 21/15 = 7/5 = 1 2/5.

[Teacher: What did you do?] First I converted the mixed number into an improper fraction, then I multiplied, then I reduced the fraction, then I went back to a mixed number.

Task: *Find 2 ÷ 5.*

Response: *[Writes]* 2 ÷ 5 = 2/1 ÷ 5/1 = 2/1 × 1/5 = 2/5. It's easiest for me to change the numbers to fractions, then divide. *[Teacher: Is there any way to check your answer?]*

I could use a calculator.   2 ÷ 5 = .4 on my calculator. I know that 2/5 = .4.

Task: *Find a fraction with a denominator of 65 that is equivalent to 9/13.*

Response: I think if I multiply both the 9 and 13 by 5, I'll get 65 on the bottom.

[Writes] 5 × 9 = 45. 5 × 13 = 65. 45/65

[Teacher: How did you know to do this?] I knew that I had to multiply the top and bottom of 9/13 by the same number, and 5 gave me 65. *[Teacher: Why do you multiply the top and bottom by the same number?]* You need to get equivalent fractions. *[Teacher: What does equivalent fractions mean?]* That you have different number of pieces but the same amount shaded.

Task: *Reduce 105/165 to simplest form.*

Response: *[Writes]* 105 ÷ 5 = 21. 165 ÷ 5 = 33. 21/33
                 21 ÷ 3 = 7. 33 ÷ 3 = 11. 7/11

[Teacher: How did you know to do this?] I just tried dividing the top and bottom by the same number. I could tell right away that 5 would work, then I divided by 3.

For strategies to help students at Level 6, see Chapter 3, page 93.

LEVEL 7: Student Uses Pictures or Materials to Solve Difficult Fraction Arithmetic Problems and to Understand More Precisely Why Symbolic Fraction Computations Work

Students at this level have a very deep understanding of fractions and fraction arithmetic that enables them to reason pictorially about difficult problems. For example, consider 3 ÷ 2/5. Students think of the problem as, "How many pieces of size 2/5 are in 3 wholes?" They then draw the picture below to determine that there are 7 1/2 copies of 2/5 in 3. So 3 ÷ 2/5 = 7 1/2.

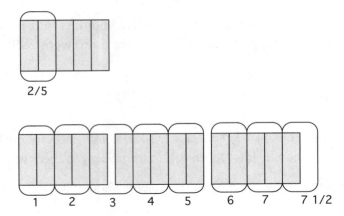

This problem is difficult to represent pictorially because 3 ÷ 2/5 is not a whole number, which makes interpretation of what happens when we try to fit the last copy of 2/5 into 3 tricky. Remember, the question is, "How many pieces of size 2/5 are in 3 wholes?" After fitting 7 whole copies of 2/5, we see that there is 1/5 left. And 1/5 is half a copy of 2/5. This kind of reasoning is considerably more difficult than pictorially solving simple problems such as 3 1/2 ÷ 1/4.

Students also understand more precisely and specifically the correspondence between computational and pictorial actions. Students using Level 6 reasoning know that to convert 2/3 into 10/15 you multiply the numerator and denominator of 2/3 by 5, and they can draw the picture below to show that their answer is correct.

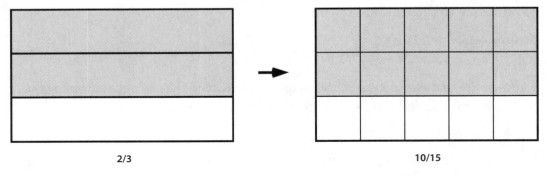

But students in Level 7 pictorially understand why the *process* of multiplying the numerator and denominator by the same number works. They understand that when we multiply the numerator and denominator of 2/3 by 5, we subdivide all the fraction pieces from 2/3 into 5 equal pieces. They also start to understand that multiplying the numerator and denominator of a fraction by the same number, like 5, is the same as multiplying the fraction by 1 because 5/5 = 1 (so their symbolic understanding is increasing too).

The specific understanding of the correspondence between computational and pictorial actions enables students to understand picture-supported, numeric explanations for why fraction computation algorithms work. For example, students can understand the following explanation for why we invert and multiply in the problem *5 ÷ 3/4*.

Think of 5 ÷ 3/4 as asking how many pieces of size 3/4 are in 5. To help us think about the problem, use the distributive property.

$$5 ÷ 3/4 = (1 + 1 + 1 + 1 + 1) ÷ 3/4$$
$$= (1 ÷ 3/4) + (1 ÷ 3/4) + (1 ÷ 3/4) + (1 ÷ 3/4) + (1 ÷ 3/4)$$

So we can solve this problem if we figure out how many 3/4s are in 1.

The picture below shows that 1 1/3 copies of 3/4 fit in 1.

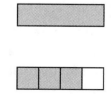

So there are 1 1/3 copies of 3/4 in each 1 of 5.

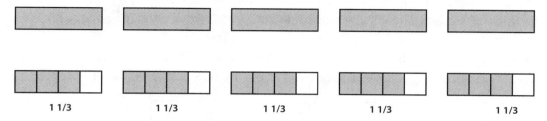

That is, there are 5 × 1 1/3 copies of 3/4 in 5. But we can write 1 1/3 as 4/3, so there are 5 × 4/3 copies of 3/4 in 5, which means that 5 ÷ 3/4 = 5 × 4/3. That is, to find 5 ÷ 3/4, we invert the divisor 3/4 and multiply: 5 × 4/3.

We can describe this reasoning symbolically, as shown below.

$$5 ÷ 3/4 = (1 + 1 + 1 + 1 + 1) ÷ 3/4$$
$$= (1 ÷ 3/4) + (1 ÷ 3/4) + (1 ÷ 3/4) + (1 ÷ 3/4) + (1 ÷ 3/4)$$
$$= 1\ 1/3 + 1\ 1/3 + 1\ 1/3 + 1\ 1/3 + 1\ 1/3$$
$$= 4/3 + 4/3 + 4/3 + 4/3 + 4/3$$
$$= 5 × 4/3$$

Other Characteristics and Illustrations of Level 7 Reasoning

Students can use graph paper to represent fraction addition and subtraction without specific guidance in the problem, and with understanding. *They can figure out how many squares to use to represent 1* (which they needed to be given at earlier levels). For instance, to add 1/3 and 1/5, students understand why the number of squares in 1 should be 15, a common denominator of the original two fractions. They can also understand why any common denominator of the original two fractions will work in solving a problem.

Note. The type of reasoning described in Level 7 is quite advanced and, without exceptional instruction, does not develop in students. In fact, most students and adults never reach Level 7. However, for students who have not attained sufficient proficiency in understanding and using formal algebraic manipulation to make genuine sense of justifications for fraction computations, they must reach Level 7. Many students in formal algebra courses struggle to attain this proficiency.

EXAMPLES

Task: *Use the graph paper below to find 1/3 + 1/5.*

Response: I need to figure out how big to make 1. I know that to add 1/3 and 1/5, I have to get fractions that have the same denominator. So I'll use 15 squares for 1 because 15 is a common denominator for thirds and fifths. *[Draws the rectangle containing 15 squares for 1.]* If I divide 1 into 3 equal pieces, I get that 1/3 is 5/15. If I divide 1 into 5 equal pieces, I get 1/5 is 3/15. This is 1/3 + 1/5 *[draws]*. So 1/3 + 1/5 equals 5/15 + 3/15, equals 8/15. *[Teacher: Why does 15 work as a common denominator?]* To make thirds, I have to be able to divide 1 into 3 equal parts *[pointing to his picture]*, so 3 has to evenly divide the number of squares in 1. To make fifths, I have to be able to divide 1 into 5 equal parts—so 5 has to evenly divide the number of squares in 1. Because I multiplied 3 and 5 together to get 15, both 3 and 5 divide 15 evenly.

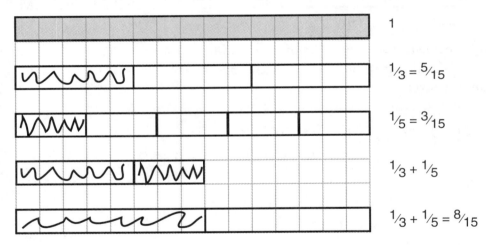

Task: *Find 2/3 × 4/5.*

Response: I'm thinking about getting 2/3 of 4/5. I know I have to divide the whole or 1 into 15 parts because I'm going to have to make thirds of fifths. If I make 3 × 5 = 15 squares, then divide 1 into 5 equal parts, there will be 3 squares in each part, so I can find thirds of fifths. So first I'll make 4/5 *[drawing and shading as shown in the second row from the top]*. Now take 2/3 of 4/5; 2 of 3 equal parts of 4/5 *[drawing and shading as in the third row from the top]*. *[Pointing at the fourth row]* So 2/3 of 4/5 is 8 squares, and that's 8/15.

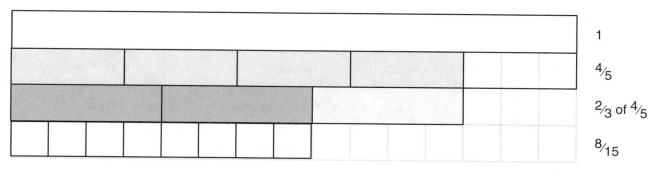

Alternatively, some students take 2/3 of each fifth in 4/5 to get 8 squares, 2 for each fifth.

Task: *To find 2/3 × 4/5, you put 2 × 4 in the numerator of the answer and 3 × 5 in the denominator. [Teacher: Why does the procedure work?]*

Response: First I shaded 4/5 [vertically], then I put [horizontal] lines to show 2/3 of 4/5. The numerator of 2/3 × 4/5 is the number of squares that are shaded and lined; 8. This is 2 × 4 because there are 2 parts lined for each of the 4 shaded sections [columns]. The denominator of 2/3 × 4/5 is 3 × 5 because I divided each of the 5 equal sections for fifths into 3 equal sections for thirds.

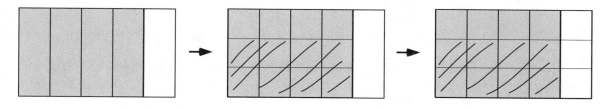

Task: *Explain why you can multiply the numerator and denominator of a fraction by the same number to create an equivalent fraction.*

Response: When you divide parts of a fraction picture into smaller equal parts, it's like multiplying. Look at the picture of 5/6.

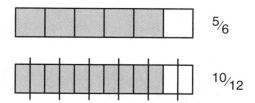

When I divide each part into 2 equal pieces, I go from 5 to 10 in the numerator, and 6 to 12 in the denominator. So I multiply the numerator and denominator by 2. If I divided each piece in 5/6 into 3 equal parts, I would multiply the numerator and denominator by 3. And so on.

Task: *Find 3/4 ÷ 2/3.*

On this graph paper I'll make 1 equal 12 squares across because 4 times 3 equals 12. So 3/4 looks like this *[third row]* and 2/3 looks like this *[fourth row]*. Now I want to know how many 2/3s are in 3/4 *[draws bottom]*. There's one 2/3 right here *[pointing to the left rectangle in the bottom row]*. And there's 1/8 of a 2/3 rectangle right here *[pointing at the square on the right side in the bottom row]*. So the answer is 1 1/8.

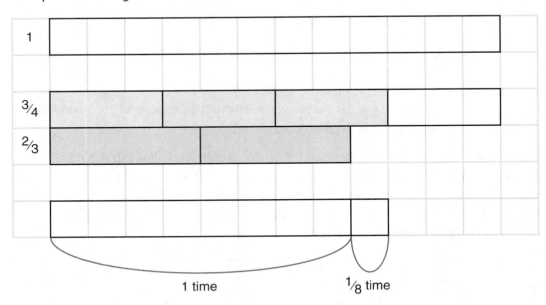

Note that 3/4 ÷ 2/3 can be interpreted a number of ways. It can be thought of as:

- How many times does 2/3 go into 3/4 [1 1/8]?
- How many ribbons of size 2/3 can be made from a ribbon of size 3/4 [one and 1/8 of a ribbon]?
- If my ruler's units are of size 2/3, how long is a ribbon of length 3/4 on this ruler?

Note that the quotient 1 1/8 tells how many *times* 2/3 goes into 3/4; it is *not* 1 1/8 of the original unit.

Task: *Find 2/31 + 4/5.*

Response: *[Writes]* $\frac{2}{31} + \frac{4}{5} = \left[\frac{2}{31} \times \frac{5}{5}\right] + \left[\frac{4}{5} \times \frac{31}{31}\right] = \frac{10}{155} + \frac{124}{155} = \frac{134}{155}$

[Teacher: Why did you multiply the first fraction by 5/5 and the second one by 31/31?] I had to convert the fractions to equivalent fractions with a common denominator so the pieces for each fraction are the same size. *[Teacher: How do you know you got equivalent fractions?]* Because in each fraction, I multiplied the top and bottom by the same number. Also because 5/5 equals 1; when you multiply a fraction by 5/5, you don't change its value.

Task: *Find a fraction with a denominator of 65 that is equivalent to 9/13.*

Response: *[Writes]* 65 ÷ 13 = 5.

$$\frac{9}{13} = \frac{9}{13} \times \frac{5}{5} = \frac{45}{65}$$

[Teacher: How did you know to do this?] I knew that I had to multiply the top and bottom of 9/13 by the same number, and when I wrote this (see below), I saw it had to be 65 on the bottom. You have to put the same number in the triangles.

$$\frac{9}{13} = \frac{\triangle \times 9}{\triangle \times 13} = \frac{45}{65}$$

It's sort of like we did in class when we changed 2/3 into 10/15. When we multiplied the numerator and denominator of 2/3 by 5, we subdivided all the fraction pieces from 2/3 into 5 equal pieces *[draws picture below]*.

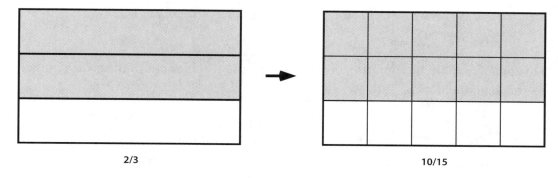

2/3   10/15

Task: *Reduce 105/165 to simplest form.*

Response: *[Writes]*

$$\frac{105}{165} = \frac{105 \div 5}{165 \div 5} = \frac{21 \div 3}{33 \div 3} = \frac{7}{11}$$

[Teacher: How did you know to do this?] You keep dividing the numerator and denominator by the same number. I did 5, then 3.

[Teacher: Why did you do it this way?] Because if you divide the numerator and denominator by the same number, you get an equivalent fraction. Like if I start with a picture of 10/15, when I divide the numerator and denominator by 5, it's like putting the 5 squares together in each row, so we get 2/3.

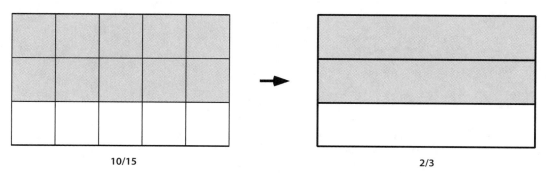

10/15   2/3

Other Properties That Can Be Justified Pictorially

In Level 7, students can understand pictorial justifications of several additional generalizations concerning operations on fractions. As students make sense of these generalizations, and describe them symbolically, they are making definite progress in moving toward algebraic reasoning. In fact, because much of the focus of Level 7 reasoning is on making sense of generalizations and processes, much of this reasoning is algebraic in nature.

Each property below is stated algebraically and in words, and a suggestion is made for how the property can be understood visually.

Property 1: $n/d = n \times 1/d$

Any fraction equals the product of its numerator and a unit fraction with its denominator.

Example: $4/5 = 4 \times 1/5$. [Visually think: 4/5 equals 4 pieces of size 1/5.]

Property 2: $n \div 1/d = n \times d$

Dividing a number by a unit fraction gives the same result as multiplying the number by the denominator.

Example: $3 \div 1/5 = 3 \times 5$. [Visually think: To find out how many 1/5s are in a number, multiply the number by 5 because there are 5 fifths in each 1.]

Property 3: $1 \div c/d = d/c$

Dividing 1 by a fraction gives the reciprocal of the fraction.

Example: $1 \div 4/7 = 7/4$

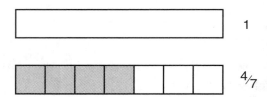

[Visually think: 1 = 1 3/4 copies of 4/7, or, if 4/7 is the measurement unit, what is the measure of 1?]

Chapter 3

Instructional Strategies for Fractions

Once you have used the assessment tasks to determine which levels of reasoning students are using, you can use the teaching suggestions and instructional tasks described in this chapter to tailor instruction to precisely fit students' learning needs. For each major level of reasoning, there are suggestions for teaching that encourage and support students' movement to the next viable type of reasoning in the sequence.

For students to make progress, have them do several problems of a specific type until you see them move to the next level, or you become convinced that they are not quite ready to move on to the next level. In the latter case, try a different kind of problem suggested for that level. (Note: For additional quality instructional activities on fractions, see Tierney, Ogonowski, Rubin, and Russell (1996).)

Teaching Students at Level 0.1: Helping Students Develop Understanding of Partitioning

For students at this level, we want to encourage and support their learning of the *process* of partitioning a set or an object into equal portions. The focus is on partitioning wholes (sets or objects) into equal portions, not determining or naming fractions. Activities should start with sets of objects that are evenly divisible by the divisor (e.g., sharing 12 candies among 2, 3, 4, or 6 people, but not among 5, 7, or 8 people). Because students often have difficulty making equal portions freehand, initial problems with whole shapes should be posed using grids.

Pose problems in a sharing context: "I have 8 cookies that I want to share equally among 4 people. Each person should get the same number of cookies. How many cookies should each person get?" When students propose solutions, always ask students how they know that each person gets the same amount. Students can show that each portion of a set consists of the same number of objects or each portion of a shape is exactly the same shape or area (perhaps by cutting pieces out). Having students cut out the parts and act out the sharing can help them understand the partitioning process.

Partitioning Sets

Initially, pose partitioning problems orally to small groups of students using physical materials. For example, you could give a group of students 12 cubes and ask them, "If 3 people share 12 cubes equally, how many cubes does each person get?" Let students work in small groups, then have groups demonstrate and describe their strategies on an overhead projector or document camera. There are numerous strategies that students can use. For instance, some students might use division: 12 ÷ 3 = 4. Some students might use trial-and-error iteration: "I make 3 groups of 3, I don't use all the cubes; so I'll try 3 groups of 4." And some students will "deal" cubes to 3 people, one at a time. Importantly, no matter what strategy students use, be sure to ask them to demonstrate how they know that each person has the same number of cubes.

After students develop fluency with easy physical partitioning problems, you can move to pictorial problems. For example, you can use the figure below from **STUDENT SHEET 1** 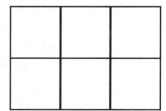 and ask, "If 3 people share 12 cookies equally, how many cookies does each person get?" (All the student sheets referenced in this chapter can be found at www.heinemann.com/products/E04345.aspx. (Click on the "Companion Resources" tab.))

Note that at first it is more difficult for students to partition objects shown in a figure than actual physical objects (because the objects in the picture cannot be physically shared).

Partitioning Shapes

Partitioning shapes requires students to break apart the whole into equal pieces. For example, you might show the diagram below and give the task, "Show how the candy bar can be shared equally by 2 people. Use a different color to show what each person gets."

Again, students may use various strategies to solve this type of problem. For instance, students can simply split the shape in half horizontally. They could think of dealing 1 square at a time to each of 2 people. Or, they might divide 6 by 2 (students using this type of numeric reasoning might color any 3 squares one color and the other 3 another color).

You could then use the same model and ask students to show how the candy bar can be shared equally by 3 people. Once students understand subdividing objects or shapes with the subdivisions already given in the materials (such as the grid lines in the "candy bar" above), you can move to partitions that require students to move beyond the given subdivisions. For example, showing how to share the candy bar equally among 4 people is more difficult because students have to further subdivide the candy bar. One way to do this is shown below. The partitioning occurs in two steps. First, each person gets one of the squares; second, each person gets one of the small rectangles. One person's share is marked with X's. The second step is typically more difficult for students.

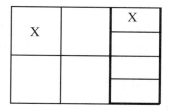

Note that at this level, we only ask students to partition the whole, *we don't ask them to determine what fraction of the whole each person gets*. So the correct answer for partitioning the candy bar into 4 parts is that each person gets 1 square and 1 small rectangle (as marked with the X's). And again, be sure to ask, "How do you know each person gets the same amount?"

The diagram that follows can be used for another type of problem. Show students the first circular region and say, "Two people want to share the pizza equally. Show how much each person gets." You can then repeat the problem for sharing among 4 people, then 3 people. Recall that the answers are drawings of partitions, not fractions. Thirds are more difficult for students to draw than halves and fourths. One way to help students solve the thirds problem is to give them several rods that are radii of the circle. They should move the rods until they find positions in which all three pieces are the same. If students divide the pizza into unequal pieces ask, "Does each person get the same amount of pizza?"

Share for 3 People

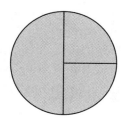

Initial Partition

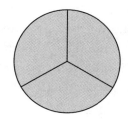

Better Partition

The problem below, from Student Sheet 1, provides a task in which more than one object must be partitioned.

Four people want to share 5 cakes equally. Show and tell how much each person gets.

Teaching Students Who Are Functioning at Level 0.2: Helping Students Develop Initial Understanding of Fractions

With students who understand partitioning but not fractions, we first introduce the concept of unit fractions, which are fractions that have 1 as their numerator (e.g., 1/2, 1/3, 1/4). The fraction $1/n$ indicates that the whole or unit has been divided into n equal pieces and we have selected 1 of these pieces. *Although it is easier for students to start understanding partitioning by working with sets of objects, it is easier for students to start understanding fractions by working with whole shapes.*

Introduce the idea of unit fractions with tasks such as, "Show how the candy bar below can be shared equally by 2 people. Shade the amount that 1 person gets." One way to conduct the discussion is to give each small group of students a single piece of paper and have them draw their solutions. The sheet of paper represents the rectangular candy bar.

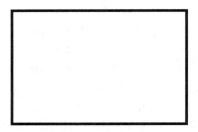

There are numerous solutions to this problem, the most common being dividing the rectangle in half horizontally, vertically, or diagonally. No matter which solution students choose, encourage them to show how the whole rectangle can be generated by 2 iterations of one of their pieces. For instance, for a horizontal split, students should show how 2 equal-sized smaller rectangles cover the whole rectangle. (It would be best to demonstrate this on a document camera or overhead projector.)

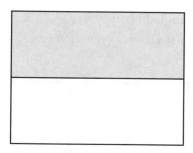

After students have correctly partitioned the candy bar into 2 equal parts, and identified how much 1 person gets, introduce fraction language and notation. "The amount that 1 person gets when the whole candy bar is shared equally between 2 people is one-half of the candy bar, the part that is shaded." Write the fraction 1/2 where students can see it, explaining, "One-half is written one over two—1 of 2 equal pieces." To keep students thinking about the critical relationship between the unit fraction and the whole, ask, "How many halves are in a whole?" Encourage students to show at least one other way that the candy bar can be partitioned into halves; one possible answer is shown below. (Note: The fraction one-half is written both vertically as $\frac{1}{2}$ and horizontally as 1/2. You should show students both ways. But you should regularly write it the way it appears in your textbook and state tests.)

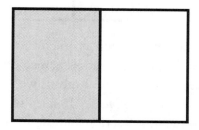

When students understand the concept of a half, you can move to other unit fractions. You can show a rectangle like the one below and ask, "How can the candy bar be shared equally by 3 people? Show what part each person gets."

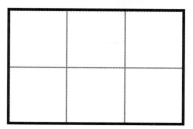

As with dividing the rectangle in half, you can show how 3 smaller rectangles can fit over the larger rectangle. This shows how the rectangle can be partitioned into 3 equal columns.

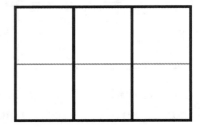

After students have correctly partitioned the candy bar into 3 equal parts, introduce fraction language and notation. "The amount that 1 person gets when the whole is equally shared between 3 people is one-third. One-third is shaded on the candy bar rectangle."

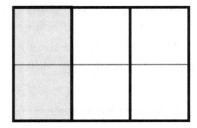

Write 1/3, saying, "One-third is written as one over three. If we divide the rectangle into 3 equal pieces, 1 of those pieces is named one-third. The 3 *[point to the 3 in 1/3]* means there are 3 equal pieces; the 1 means we take 1 of those pieces *[point to the 1 in 1/3]*; 1/3 means 1 of 3 equal pieces." To keep students thinking about the critical relationship between the unit fraction and the whole, ask, "How many thirds are in a whole?"

You can use similar examples to show other unit fractions, such as one-sixth. For instance, in the first problem on **STUDENT SHEET 2** , students are asked to show how the candy bar below can be shared equally by 6 people, and to shade the amount that 1 person gets.

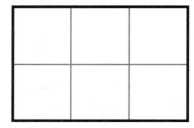

To encourage students to see that the whole consists of 6 iterations of a square, show the grid, then show on an overhead or document camera how 6 squares cover the rectangle (you can use a 3 inch by 2 inch rectangle and plastic inch squares).

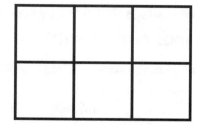

After students have correctly partitioned the candy bar into 6 equal parts, introduce fraction language and notation. "The amount that 1 person gets when the whole is equally shared between 6 people is one-sixth. One-sixth is written one over six (write 1/6). What does the 6 mean? What does the 1 mean? How many sixths are in a whole?"

Have students complete Student Sheet 2 to see how well they understand the ideas in the above discussion. Have students explain their answers in a class discussion.

Introducing Non-Unit Fractions

Once students have a firm understanding of unit fractions, help them understand non-unit fractions. For example, give students the model below and ask, "The candy bar has been divided up so that it can be shared equally by 8 people. Shade the amount that 3 people get."

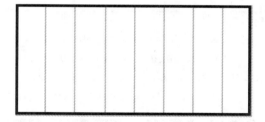

After students have correctly shaded the candy bar, introduce fraction language and notation. Write 3/8 and tell students, "The shaded amount is three-eighths, which is written three over eight—3 of 8 equal pieces; 8 people are sharing the whole equally, and we have shaded the amount for 3 people."

You can then repeat the exercise for other amounts, such as 5/8: "The candy bar has been divided so it can be shared equally by 8 people. Shade the amount that 5 people get." As before, introduce the fraction language and notation after students have correctly shaded the diagram. Then continue by asking students to shade 7/8 of the bar, and ask, "How do you know this is 7/8?" Students can continue this reasoning with problems like those on **STUDENT SHEET 3** . After students complete the sheet, have a class discussion similar to the one described above. Use an overhead projector or document camera to show the models.

You can help students develop understanding of the relationship between unit fractions and non-unit fractions by asking questions such as, "How many 1/8 are in the whole? How many 1/8 are in 7/8? How many 1/8 are in 3/8?"

Teaching Students at Levels 1 and 2: Moving to Iterating and Partitioning Shapes and Quantities

After introducing the concept of fractions to students, we give activities to help them visually understand the fraction-creation process—Level 3. However, even though Level 3 is our goal, most students will pass through Level 2 reasoning (and some through Levels 1 and 2) before getting to Level 3. So, although we do not intentionally attempt to get students to Levels 1 and 2, recognize that inevitably many students will pass through these levels. Also, on many of the instructional tasks that encourage Level 3 reasoning, some students will use Level 4 reasoning. At this time, be sure that all students understand Level 3 reasoning. But if students offer Level 4 solutions, including these solutions in the class discussion can help students start building Level 4 reasoning from Level 3 reasoning.

To build Level 3 reasoning, you can work on tasks such as those on **STUDENT SHEET 4** . One such task and suggested discussion is shown below.

Shade each black rectangle below to show one-half (1/2) in a different way. Tell how you know that one-half of the black rectangle is shaded.

One way that students use Level 3 reasoning on this task is when they draw a single segment that divides the rectangle into congruent shapes (note that there are numerous ways to do this). Be sure to ask students to demonstrate that their subdivision of the rectangle produces 2 congruent or equal parts.

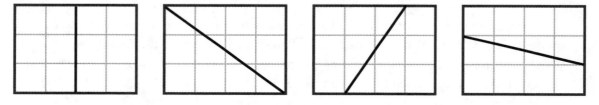

Another way for students to use Level 3 reasoning on this task is to shade 6 squares and argue that these shaded squares can be moved to form a rectangle that is one-half of the black rectangle (see shaded parts below).

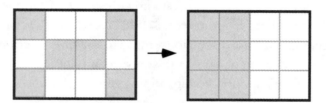

Students use Level 4 reasoning on this task when they argue that there are 12 squares in the rectangle, so any shading with 6 squares is one-half. One way to help students at Level 3 make sense of this Level 4 reasoning is to have them think about rearranging the squares as shown above.

As students develop Level 3 reasoning, we want to encourage them to use and abstract the *process* of iterating a part to make a whole as a way of establishing part-to-whole relationships with fractions. Pattern blocks allow students to do the iteration physically. In pattern block tasks such as those on **STUDENT SHEETS 5–8**, we focus on unit fractions, and we ask students what fraction a given pattern block is of a whole made up of one or more pattern blocks. Students determine the answer by making the whole from the part (that is, iterating the part to make the whole). The number of iterations determines the size of the fractional part. For example, because 4 iterations of the rhombus pattern block make the whole shape below, 1 rhombus is 1/4 of the whole shape.

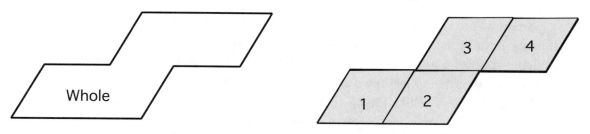

Because the whole keeps changing in the pattern block activities, the focus is on the relationship between the fractional part and the whole.

Understanding the Non-Unit Fraction Creation Process

After students have proficiency creating unit fractions, encourage them to develop an understanding of how non-unit fractions are created. For instance, in one task from **STUDENT SHEET 9**, students are asked to shade the black rectangle below to show two-thirds (2/3) of the rectangle in different ways.

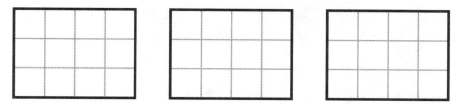

One way that students use Level 3 reasoning on this task is when they draw two segments that divide the rectangle into 3 congruent shapes (see two ways of doing this below). Be sure to ask students to demonstrate that their subdivision of the rectangle produces 3 congruent or equal parts. (Note that students' drawing of the figure on the right is approximate.)

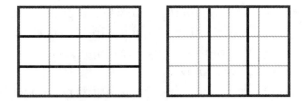

Another way for students to use Level 3 reasoning on this task is to shade 8 squares and argue that these shaded squares can be moved to form a rectangle that is two-thirds of the black rectangle (see shaded parts below).

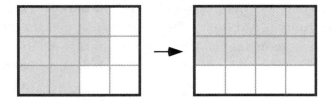

Students use Level 4 reasoning on this task when they argue that there are 12 squares in the rectangle, so any shading with 8 squares is two-thirds. One way to help students at Level 3 make sense of this Level 4 reasoning is to have them think about rearranging the squares as shown above.

Pattern block tasks like the one below and on **STUDENT SHEETS 10–14** 🔽 can help students focus on using iteration to identify non-unit fractions. In these tasks, students predict what fraction of each picture is shaded, then check by iterating pattern blocks. For instance, the picture on the right below shows that 4/6 of the hexagonal shape on the left is shaded because the triangle can be iterated 6 times to make the hexagon and 4 times to make the shaded portion of the hexagon.

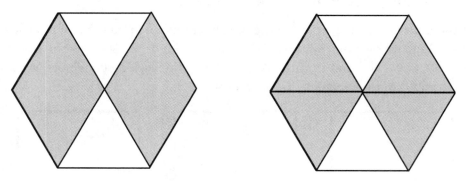

In tasks such as these, encourage students to predict an answer, check with pattern blocks, then explain their answers. As shown for the above example, they can use a pattern block to explain an answer by iterating the block to find the whole shape (the number of these iterations is the fraction denominator), and then iterate the shape to find the shaded part (the number of these iterations is the numerator of the fraction).

Another useful type of task asks students to figure out how to divide a whole into equal pieces in order to determine the fraction of the whole that is shaded (see **STUDENT SHEET 15**) 🔽 . For instance, consider the problem below of determining the fraction of the large square that is shaded.

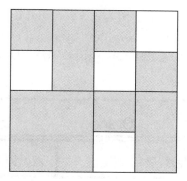

To do this, students have to figure out what kind of piece will cover the whole shape a whole number of times and will also cover the shaded part a whole number of times. By dividing the large square into small squares as shown below, we can see that the shaded part is 12/16 of the whole square.

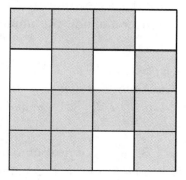

Additionally, we can see by arranging the little squares or by dividing the numerator and denominator of 12/16 by 4 that another fractional name for the shaded part is 3/4. That is, 12/16 is equivalent to 3/4.

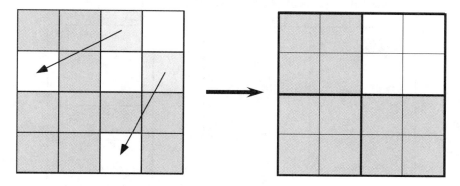

Cuisenaire Rods Fractions

Cuisenaire rods are another useful tool for developing fraction understanding. Consider this problem (found on **STUDENT SHEET 16**) :

Find 1/5 if the orange rod is 1. Prove it is 1/5. [Use Cuisenaire rods.]

To solve this problem, students have to find a rod that can be iterated 5 times to make the orange rod, which they accomplish by visual estimation and testing. As is shown below, the red rod can be iterated 5 times to make the orange rod, so the red rod is 1/5 of the orange rod.

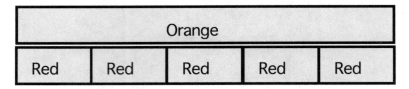

Focusing on the Unit

Because students have so much difficulty maintaining the unit as they deal with fractions, it is important to discuss this issue explicitly. Problems like the one below can be the basis of an explicit discussion of how the amount represented by a fraction is determined by what the unit is.

> *Jonathan ate 1/2 of a pizza. Emily ate 1/2 of another pizza. Jonathan said that he ate more pizza than Emily. But Emily said they both ate the same amount of pizza because they both ate 1/2. Use words and pictures to show who could be right.*

Students might use various CBA levels of reasoning on this task, all of which should be shared in a class discussion. At Levels 1 and 2, students think Jonathan and Emily ate the same amount because they think that all halves are the same. At Level 3 students say that Jonathan could be right because the pizzas could have been different sizes (they could draw a picture like the one below). For all these students, it is critical to demonstrate the ideas pictorially.

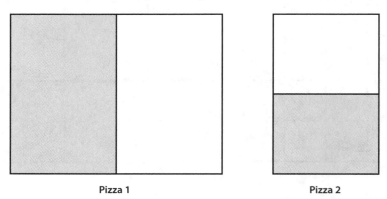

Pizza 1   Pizza 2

When considering students' reasoning about this task, it is critical to recall our discussion in Chapter 1 about units. When we are talking about 1/2 of something—like pizzas, or sets of cupcakes, or even numbers (1/2 of 10 versus 1/2 of 30)—1/2 may be unequal to 1/2 because it is 1/2 of one thing versus 1/2 of a different thing. So be careful with language. Whenever you refer to 1/2 "of something," be sure to include the something in the reference—say, "one-half of Pizza 1," not "one-half."

Teaching Students at Level 3: Moving to Iterating and Partitioning Quantities in Multiple Contexts

The activities in the previous section—which utilize different shapes as the whole and different sets of materials—not only help students move to Level 3 but also help move them toward Level 4. The activities in this section specifically focus on getting students to understand the fraction creation process in multiple contexts as a way for them to develop Level 4 reasoning about *quantities*. Students think about iterating quantities rather than shapes. Even when they iterate shapes, they think of them in terms of quantities, like their area or volume.

Fractions of Sets of Objects

Problems such as those on **STUDENT SHEETS 17–20** help students develop an understanding of the process of finding fractions of sets of objects. Student Sheets 17–19 encourage students to use physical materials like multilink or unifix cubes, first for unit fractions, then for non-unit fractions. Student Sheet 20 encourages students to use pictorial solutions. (Of course, students can also use drawing on Student Sheets 17–19.)

When students begin finding fractions of sets of objects, encourage them to determine and justify their answers using iteration or partitioning of physical objects. For instance, students can show that 1/2 of 12 cubes is 6 by grouping the cubes as shown below.

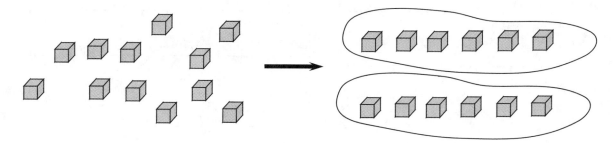

Students might say that 2/3 of 12 cubes is 8 cubes by grouping the cubes as shown below and justify their work by saying, "Twelve cubes is the whole, which I made into one rod. Then divide the whole into 3 equal sets of 4 cubes; so 4 cubes is 1/3 of 12 cubes. That makes 2/3 of 12 cubes 8 cubes."

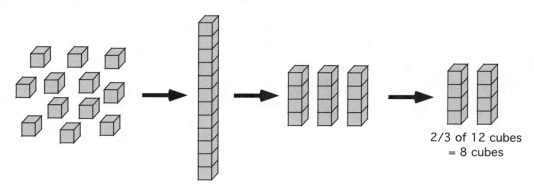

2/3 of 12 cubes
= 8 cubes

The middle part of the diagram explicitly connects partitioning the set of 12 cubes to the partitioning reasoning students use when the whole is a single object, such as a geometric shape. Making this connection explicit can be quite helpful for students who are struggling to extend their fraction reasoning from single shapes (like a rectangle or circle) to sets of objects.

Number Lines

Number lines are another important representation for fractions. We want to help students extend their knowledge of the iteration process for creating fractions to number lines. For instance, suppose students are asked to name the fraction marked by X on the number line.

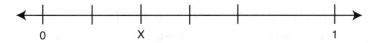

First, students must understand that the segment between 0 and 1 on the number line should be partitioned into equal sections. So students must understand that counting hash marks or unequal segments is incorrect. For example, by counting hash marks, the first student says that X is at 3/6, and by counting unequal segments, the second student says that X is at 2/5. In contrast, the third student iterates equal segments to see that X is at 2/6, and the fourth student iterates larger equal segments to see that X is at 1/3.

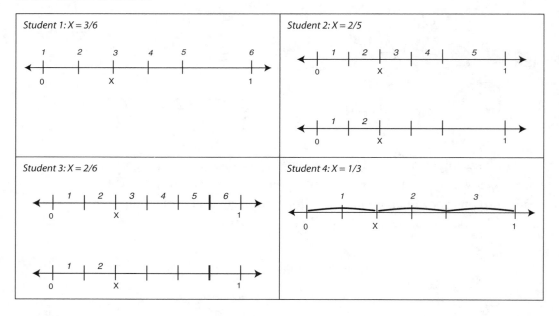

Ask students questions that promote iterative reasoning. "What size segment can I repeat so that I divide the segment between 0 and 1 into equal parts? How many equal parts will I get *[6]*? How many of these segments do I have to repeat to get from 0 to X *[2]*? So what fraction tells where X is located *[2/6]*?" **STUDENT SHEET 21** gives students an opportunity to construct this reasoning.

Equivalent Fractions

We want to help students solidify their intuitive visual notion of equivalent fractions and to move to a quantitative numerical conception of this important idea. For instance, on the first problem of **STUDENT SHEET 22** , we ask students to "Shade 1/2 of the rectangle in different ways to show that 1/2 = 2/4 = 3/6 = 4/8 = 6/12 = 12/24."

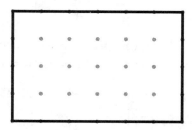

Students can partition the rectangle as follows to show these equivalences visually.

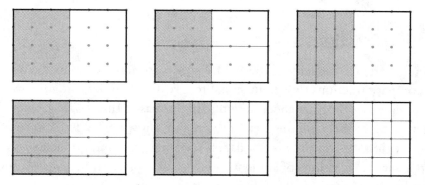

Be sure to ask, "How are these shadings alike? *[They each contain 12 one-by-one squares, which is half the area of the rectangle.]*"

In the second problem on Student Sheet 22, students show equivalence by shading and grouping a set of 12 cubes in different ways. They are to show that 2/3 = 4/6 = 8/12.

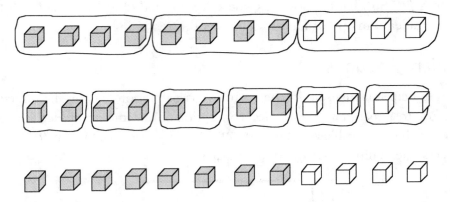

If students have difficulty doing this problem with pictures, have them use multilink cubes of different colors and link the cubes within each set together.

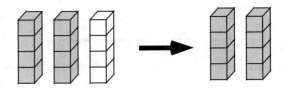

Comparing Fractions

To continue students' movement toward Level 4 reasoning, we want to encourage them to compare fractions (less than, equal to, greater than) by using *numerical analysis* of quantities. For instance, students might reason that 1/2 is greater than 1/3 in the picture below because the area of the region showing 1/2 is 12 squares and the area of the region showing 1/3 is 8 squares. You might encourage such reasoning by asking appropriate questions of students who are using strictly visual reasoning (such as "1/2 looks bigger than 1/3"). Ask, "How do you know for sure that 1/2 is greater than 1/3? Can counting squares help? If you count squares, what fraction of the left rectangle is shaded *[12/24]*? What fraction of the right rectangle is shaded *[8/24]*? So which is larger and why?"

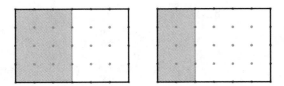

As another example, consider the question, "Which is bigger, 5/12 or 11/24? Use the rectangles below to find an answer."

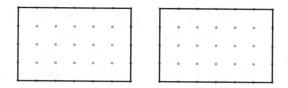

On this problem, encourage reasoning in which students partition the rectangles so that they have a common denominator: "5/12 is 10 squares, so it's 10/24; 11/24 is 11 squares; so 11/24 is bigger."

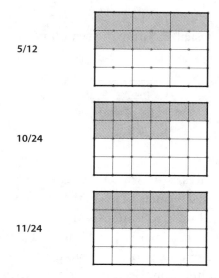

5/12

10/24

11/24

Encourage this type of reasoning by having students work on **STUDENT SHEET 23.**

Encouraging Numerical Fraction Reasoning

A key element of Level 4 reasoning is understanding that fractions can be determined quantitatively (rather than visually). For example, in Level 4, a student can reason that half the large square below is shaded because 8 of the small squares are shaded and 8 are not shaded. **STUDENT SHEET 24** further promotes this type of reasoning.

Although some students seem to arrive at this type of quantitative reasoning by logical deduction (they just see it must be true), many more students will come to believe in this type of reasoning by reflecting on repeated experiences with visual material.

For instance, as shown below, you can build on students' use of Level 3 visual reasoning to help them understand that because 8 out of 16 equal squares are shaded in the above shape, one-half of the shape is shaded. If you slide each of the lightly shaded squares on the right side of the shape to the left, you make a shape that is divided into 2 equal parts. So half of the shape is shaded. Iteration can be done both visually (each of the halves can be iterated 2 times to make the whole shape), and numerically (8 iterated 2 times—8, 16—makes 16). The numeric iteration shows that any set of 8 squares in the large square is one-half of the large square.

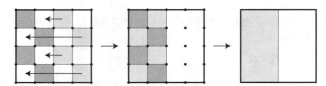

A similar combination of visual and numeric reasoning shows that 3/4 of the figure below is shaded.

First, move the 3 dark squares as shown on the left. Then use visual iteration: the 2-by-2 square can be iterated 4 times to make the whole shape, 3 times to make the shaded part. Numerically, 4 iterated 4 times—4, 8, 12, 16—makes 16 (the whole shape); 4 iterated 3 times—4, 8, 12—makes 12 (the shaded part); so 3/4 of the whole shape is shaded. Note that the middle part of the picture below shows the connection between visual and numerical iteration. Each iteration of a 2-by-2 square iterates 4 squares. Note that this reasoning can be used to show that any set of 12 little squares is 3/4 of the large square.

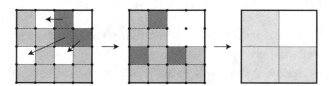

Many students needed repeated experiences with this combination of visual and numerical reasoning to understand that to find the fraction represented by the picture, all they have to do is count the total number of little squares and the number of little squares that are shaded.

Note that this type of visual-numerical reasoning also promotes (a) understanding of equivalent fractions [3/4 = 12/16], and (b) finding fractions of sets and numbers [3/4 of 16 = 12].

Reversing the Fraction Creation Process

An essential type of reasoning that develops in Level 4 is understanding the fraction creation process via iteration and partitioning well enough to reverse the process. That is, the fraction creation process creates a fractional part from the whole; the reverse process creates the whole from the fractional part.

To illustrate the reasoning required for these problems, consider the problem below.

If this rod is 3/4, find the rod that is 1.

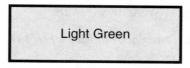

To solve this problem, think about the process, the sequence of steps, of creating 3/4.

Step 1: Select a rod to be 1.

Step 2. Find a rod that can be iterated 4 times to make the 1 rod. This is 1/4 of 1.

Step 3. Iterate the 1/4 rod 3 times to make 3/4 of the original whole.

We want to reverse this process.

Step 1. Find a rod that can be iterated 3 times to make the 3/4 rod. As shown below, the white rod can be iterated 3 times to make the 3/4 light green rod. Because the light green rod is 3/4, the white rod must be the 1/4 rod.

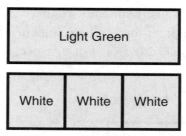

Step 2. We know that there are four 1/4 rods in 1, so iterate the 1/4 rod 4 times to get the 1 rod. Since the purple rod matches 4 copies of the white rod, the purple rod must be the 1 rod.

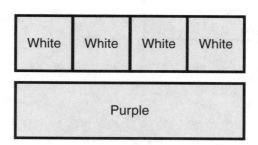

To check your reasoning, note that if the purple rod is 1, then the white rod is 1/4 because 4 copies of the white rod make the purple rod. Because 3 copies of the white rod make the light green rod, the light green rod is 3/4 of the purple rod.

STUDENT SHEETS 25–28 ⬇ provide a wide variety of problems that can promote this kind of reasoning in a variety of contexts. If students have difficulty, ask guiding questions that help students focus on the processes described above. For instance, if students are unable to create 1 when they are given a piece that is 1/5, ask them, "If I had a whole or 1, how would I find 1/5 *[divide 1 into 5 equal pieces]*? How many 1/5s would be in 1 *[5]*? So, if this rod is 1/5, how do I make 1 *[make 5 copies]*?"

To promote this type of reasoning as applied to sets of objects, consider how it can be applied to Problem 5 on Student Sheet 28:

> *Jon ate 12 cookies. That was 3/4 of the whole bag of cookies. How many cookies were in the whole bag?*

The problem tells us that if we take 3/4 of some unknown number of cookies, we get 12 cookies. That means that if we divide the unknown set of cookies into 4 equal groups, then select 3 of those groups, we get 12 cookies. So, think backwards; reverse this process. 12 is 3 equal groups of how many cookies *[4]*? And 4 equal groups of 4 cookies is what *[16 cookies]*? So 3/4 of 16 cookies is 12 cookies.

Some students may need to do this problem concretely, so make cubes (or some other suitable counters) available.

Dealing with Improper Fractions

Students often have difficulty understanding improper fractions. It is difficult for them to conceive of a fraction that represents more than the whole. As they begin to work with improper fractions, many students will need help in keeping track of the whole. Reasoning with visual iteration can help students think about these problems (such as those on **STUDENT SHEET 29**) ⊕. For instance, consider the following problem.

The rectangle is 1. Show 5/2.

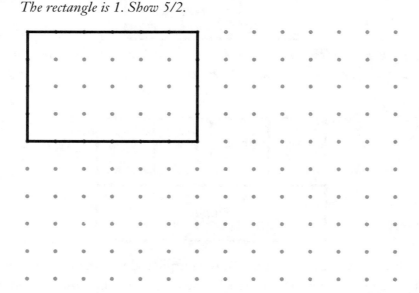

First, use partitioning to establish what 1/2 looks like.

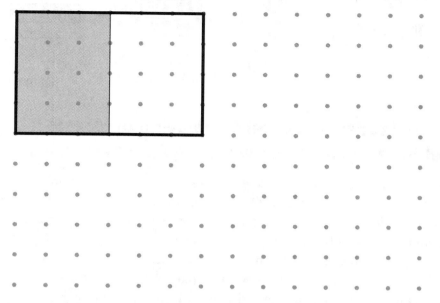

Second, iterate 1/2 five times to find 5/2. Group the halves into wholes. The shaded part is 5/2 of the original rectangle.

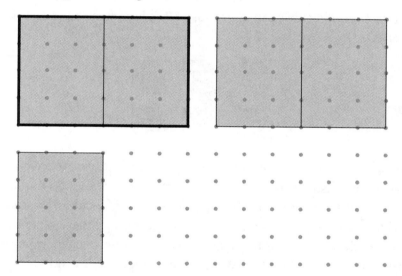

Note that when finding improper fractions of sets of cubes (see **STUDENT SHEET 30**), it can be very helpful for students to snap cubes together in ways that use the type of reasoning just demonstrated for the rectangle above. For instance, consider the problem, "How many cubes are in 3/2 of a bag of 12 cubes?" (See the figure below.) In the first step, the student can snap cubes together in a way that establishes 1/2 of 12 cubes. In the second step, the student iterates 1/2 three times, showing that there 18 cubes is 3/2 of 12 cubes.

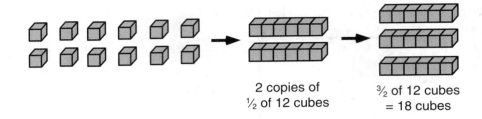

2 copies of
½ of 12 cubes

³⁄₂ of 12 cubes
= 18 cubes

Teaching Students at Level 4.1: Moving to Mental Model-Based Numerical Reasoning About Fractions

Whenever you are doing activities to encourage Level 4 thought, think of encouraging Level 4.1 pictorial (or physical) reasoning about fractional quantities first. Once students develop some proficiency with Level 4.1 reasoning pictorially, then have them try to do problems in the same context mentally, by imagining situations. Revisiting this "pictures first, imagination second" sequence in each context will help students develop the more abstract reasoning required in Level 4.2.

More specifically, to encourage and support Level 4.2 reasoning, ask questions to help students reflect on what they are doing in ways that build conceptual understanding. For instance, to answer the question, "What is 2/3 of 6 cubes?" a student might separate a set of 6 cubes into 3 groups of 2 cubes, then select 2 of the sets, getting 4 cubes.

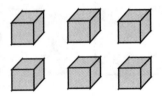

As students repeatedly do the cube problems, with appropriate encouragement, they will eventually abstract the process so that they can operate on numbers rather than cubes. For instance, for the problem, "What is 2/3 of 6 cubes?" a student might think "6 divided into 3 equal sets puts 2 in each set, and 2 of these sets makes 4. So 2/3 of 6 is 4." So the student has moved from visual to numerical reasoning.

The problems on **STUDENT SHEET 31** ⊕ encourage the transition from Level 4.1 to Level 4.2. For instance, for the problem, "2/3 of X cubes," first we let X be 3, then 6, then 12, then 24. Repeating and writing a description of the procedure helps students abstract the procedure—that is, form a mental model of it. As a follow-up, after students have completed Problems 1–4 on Student Sheet 31, ask them (Problem 5), "What is 3/8 of 40?" Students should imagine that 40 can be divided into 8 equal sets of 5; 3 of these sets is 15. *So 3/8 of 40 is 15.*

Imagining cubes instead of actually manipulating them moves students one step closer to abstract reasoning on numbers. If students have difficulty, however, you might show them the picture of 40 cubes in an 8 by 5 array for 5 seconds and ask if that helps. If that does not help, let the students inspect the image for as long as they need to. Repeated requests to imagine the situation (without pictures) will encourage appropriate abstraction of image-based mental models that enable students to operate on images mentally.

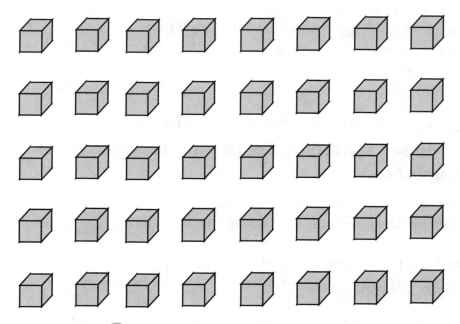

STUDENT SHEET 32 🔽 can also help with this abstraction process. It asks students to find 3/5 of 15 in five different contexts: linking cubes, graph paper, a student-generated drawing, Cuisenaire rods, and a number line. What the process has in common in these different contexts is, in essence, the abstraction we are trying to promote.

Toward the end of Level 4, you can have students use Level 4.2 reasoning to rethink problems on several previous student sheets. For instance, consider the problem from Student Sheet 28:

> *Jon ate 12 cookies. That was 3/4 of the whole bag of cookies. How many cookies were in the whole bag?*

As students work on this problem, encourage Level 4.2 reasoning by asking them to write numbers to help them mentally visualize it, saying, "The problem tells us that when we take 3/4 of some number, we get 12. *[You might write on the board, 3/4 of ☐ = 12.]* Now think of 12 objects. How do we find 3/4 of a set of 12 objects? *[We divide the objects into 4 equal groups, then select 3 of those groups.]* Now, think backwards; reverse this process. 12 is 3 equal groups of what number *[4]*? And 4 equal groups of 4 is what *[16]*? So 3/4 of 16 is 12."

Or consider this more challenging problem:

> *Mario ate 40 jelly beans. That was 5/8 of the whole bag of jelly beans. Naomi ate 1/4 of the whole bag of jelly beans. How many jelly beans did Naomi eat? What fraction of the whole bag of jelly beans was left?*

Help guide students to the following reasoning: The problem tells us that if we take 5/8 of the whole bag of jelly beans, we get 40. That means that if we divide the whole bag of jelly beans into 8 equal groups, then select 5 of those groups, we get 40 jelly beans. So, think backwards; reverse this process. 40 is 5 equal groups of what number *[8]*? So what is 1/8 of the whole bag of jelly beans *[8]*? So how many were in the whole bag of jelly beans *[8 equal groups of 8 is 64]*? So there are 64 jelly beans in the whole bag. What is 1/4 of 64 *[16]*? So Naomi ate 16 jelly beans. The total number of jelly beans eaten is 40 for Mario + 16 for Naomi = 56. So there are 8 jelly beans left, or 1/8 of the whole bag.

Teaching Students at Level 4.2: Moving to Developing Image-Based Reasoning About Arithmetic Operations on Simple Fractions

Activities in this section help students develop the image-based reasoning they need to perform arithmetic operations on simple fractions.

Promoting Understanding of Fraction Equivalence and Comparison

Students must be proficient in recognizing and creating equivalent fractions to reason conceptually about addition and subtraction of fractions. To encourage this facility, have students use graph paper to find equivalent fractions and compare fractions, as on **STUDENT SHEET 33** . For instance, asked to draw three fractions equivalent to 1/2 using a given grid, students can draw the following that shows that 1/2 = 2/4 = 3/6 = 6/12:

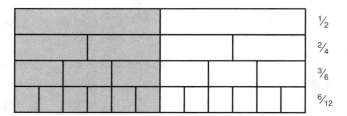

For comparing fractions, give tasks like those on **STUDENT SHEET 34** . Students are asked to use the rectangle on the left to show which fraction is larger by converting 5/6 and 3/4 to equivalent fractions with the same denominator. Help students create pictures like those below to show that 3/4 = 9/12 and 5/6 = 10/12, so 5/6 > 3/4.

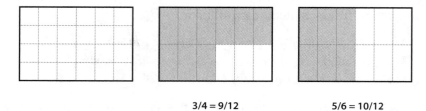

3/4 = 9/12   5/6 = 10/12

Promoting Understanding of Fraction Addition and Subtraction

To add or subtract fractions, students must first find a common denominator, but before that it is important for them to see *why* they need common denominators. **STUDENT SHEET 35** encourages students to see why they need common denominators by asking them to analyze incorrect student work, such as the following:

> *Asked to find 1/4 + 1/3, Harriet drew the picture below and said, "This is 1/4 [top]. This is 1/3 [middle]. Put 1/4 and 1/3 together [bottom]. So the answer is 2/3."*

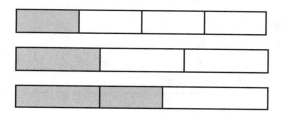

To help students see that they need a common denominator, have them recall what a fraction means. For instance, to find 2/3 of a shape, we divide the shape into 3 *equal* parts and take 2 of the parts. So in the diagram above, the part that is shaded in the bottom line is clearly not 2/3 because the 2 shaded pieces are not equal.

Only by dividing the whole into equal pieces that will fit into both fourths and thirds can we see what fraction of the whole is shaded. A common denominator for 1/4 and 1/3 is 1/12. So the shaded portion of the bottom line is 7/12.

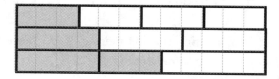

Once students understand the role of common denominators, encourage them to develop concrete ways to add and subtract fractions. **STUDENT SHEETS 36 AND 37** provide some problems that can help students develop their understanding. Note that there are three types of problems for both addition and subtraction: (1) the two fractions to be added/subtracted have a common denominator; (2) the denominator of one fraction can serve as the common denominator; (3) the product of the denominators can serve as a common denominator. Note that students need to do several problems of each type to develop understanding and proficiency with these problems. Two sample problems are shown below.

To add 1/3 and 1/5, students who understand adding fractions with unlike denominators can reason that 1/3 is 5/15 and 1/5 is 3/15, so 1/3 + 1/5 = 8/15.

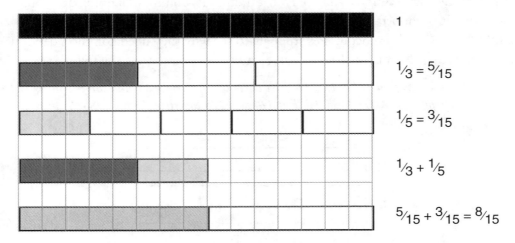

For students having some difficulty, you can guide them through the process with questions. For instance, reconsider the problem 1/3 + 1/5, shown above. You can use a sequence of questions such as the following to help students understand the situation and how to solve the problem.

- What is the unit or 1? *[the black rectangle]*
- Draw 1/3 on the grid. How do you know it is 1/3? *[There are 3 equal pieces and I shaded 1.]*
- Draw 1/5 on the grid. How do you know it is 1/5? *[There are 5 equal pieces and I shaded 1.]*
- If I add 1/3 and 1/5 by putting the 1/3 piece and 1/5 piece together, what do I get? *[2 pieces]* Are they the same size? Is this 2/3? *[No, it's not 2/3 because the pieces are not the same size.]*
- Is there any way to divide the 1/3 and 1/5 into the same size pieces? *[You can use the squares.]*
- What fraction is 1 square? *[1/15 because 15 squares make 1]*
- How many 15ths is 1/3? *[5]* How many 15ths is 1/5? *[3]* How many 15ths is 1/3 plus 1/5? *[8]* So what fraction is 1/3 + 1/5? *[8/15]*
- How is the 15 related to 1/3 and 1/5? *[3 × 5 = 15]* What is a common denominator for 1/3 and 1/5? *[15ths]*

It is important to note that this visually presented problem helps students find a common denominator by predividing 1 into 15 squares.

Students can do subtraction problems in a way similar to how they did addition; they need to get a common denominator (which is suggested by the grid given with the problem). To subtract 1/5 from 1/3, students reason that 1/3 is 5/15 and 1/5 is 3/15, so 1/3 − 1/5 = 2/15.

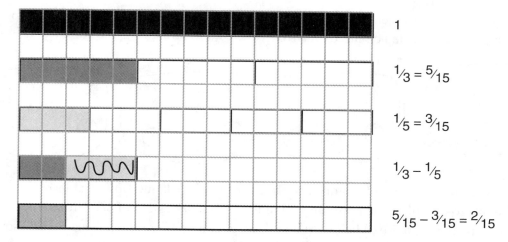

1

$1/3 = 5/15$

$1/5 = 3/15$

$1/3 - 1/5$

$5/15 - 3/15 = 2/15$

Once students understand the problems like those on Student Sheets 36 and 37, you can present problems in which they use graph paper to solve the problem but the problems do not show how 1 should be chosen on the graph paper. For instance, for the problem 2/3 + 1/4, if students do not know where to start, ask, "How should we draw 1 on the graph paper? How does knowing a common denominator help us figure out how to draw 1? What should we use for a common denominator for 2/3 and 1/4? *[12ths]* So how many squares should be in 1? *[12]*"

Additional problems for doing addition and subtraction of fractions pictorially and concretely are given on **STUDENT SHEETS 38–40** ⬇ .

Promoting Understanding of Fraction Multiplication and Division

Multiplication

The primary way to think of multiplication at a physical-conceptual level is to see multiplication in terms of groups or portions "of" some set or quantity. For whole numbers, we might think of 3 × 4 as 3 groups of 4. For fractions, we can think of 3/4 × 24 as 3/4 *of* 24. To find 3/4 *of* 24, think about separating 24 objects into 4 equal groups by dividing 24 by 4 to get 6 in each group; then find the total in 3 groups (which is 18). Note that finding 3/4 × 24 = 3/4 *of* 24 is like finding 3/4 if the whole is a set of 24 objects.

As a different example, you can think of 3 × 2 1/2 as 3 groups of 2 1/2, which we can envision as 3 groups of 2, which is 6, and 3 groups of 1/2, which is 1 1/2. So the total is 6 + 1 1/2 = 7 1/2.

Problems like those on **STUDENT SHEET 41** ⬇ can help you encourage this type of reasoning by having students find solutions to fraction multiplication problems using drawings. The problems on this sheet are constructed so that visual solutions are straightforward. For instance, for the problem 3/4 × 24, ask questions that lead students to the following reasoning. "Think of 3/4 × 24 as 3/4 *of* 24." To do this, students can draw 24 circles, loop 4 groups of 6 circles, shade the circles in 3 groups, then count the shaded circles to get 18.

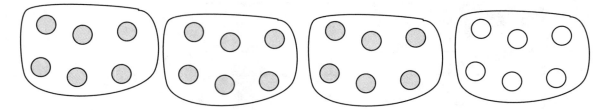

As a different kind of example, consider 2/3 × 6/7. Ask questions that lead students to the following reasoning. "Think of 2/3 × 6/7 as 2/3 of 6/7." To do this, draw a picture of 6/7 (see below). Then think of taking 2/3 of the 6 pieces in 6/7, so loop 3 groups of 2 of these pieces. Shade 2 of these 3 groups in a different way to see that there are 4 pieces of size 1/7 in 2/3 of 6/7. So 2/3 × 6/7 = 4/7.

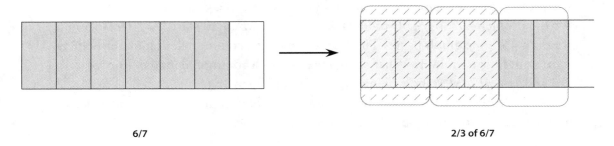

6/7   2/3 of 6/7

Division

There are two kinds of physical reasoning about division problems. Students need to understand both types of reasoning and to recognize which type of reasoning is appropriate in various situations.

Measurement reasoning asks how many copies of the divisor are in the dividend. For instance, to reason about 2 1/2 ÷ 1/4 we can ask how many fourths are in 2 1/2, which students might do with pictures or mentally.

Response 1: *This is 2 1/2 divided into fourths. There are 10 fourths in 2 1/2.*

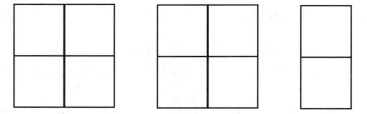

Response 2 *[mentally]***:** *There are 4 fourths in 1, so 8 fourths in 2. And there are 2 fourths in 1/2. So there are 8 + 2 equals 10 fourths in 2 1/2.*

To encourage students to move from pictures to mental computation, after they are proficient with drawing pictures, give new problems and ask them if they can do the problems mentally, visualizing what should happen. If they can't visualize, let them draw pictures, then ask them again if they can picture what they drew when their eyes are closed. Then have them try more problems using visualization. With repeated attempts at visualizing, students will abstract the process so that they can perform it mentally. Gradually, with repeated application of mental imagery, the imagery will transform into mental models for manipulation of fraction quantities (as demonstrated in Response 2).

Partitive reasoning asks, "If the dividend is partitioned (divided) into a number of equal parts equal to the divisor, how much is in each part?" For instance, a student might solve the problem 4 1/2 ÷ 2 by dividing 4 1/2 into 2 equal parts by drawing the picture below and circling the part that one person gets, saying that each person gets 2 1/4.

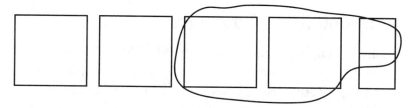

Like Student Sheet 41 for multiplication, **STUDENT SHEET 42** provides opportunities for you to first encourage and support students' development of mental imagery, then more abstract mental model reasoning about division of fractions.

Additional problems for doing fraction arithmetic pictorially and concretely are given on **STUDENT SHEETS 43 AND 44.**

Teaching Students at Level 5: Moving to Meaningful Use of Symbolic Fraction Computation

The goal of activities in this section is for students to learn algorithms for fraction arithmetic in a way that makes some intuitive sense to them. Students do not have sufficient understanding of algebra to make sense of algebraic justifications of the algorithms. And they do not understand the pictorial procedures for fraction arithmetic deeply enough to connect pictorial and symbolic actions. So, because students have achieved Level 5 reasoning, we have them solve sets of problems pictorially and look for symbolic patterns in the solved problems. This helps students see that the symbolic manipulations are consistent with the pictorial arithmetic they have already made sense of. Indeed, it is critical for students to see a connection between their intuitive ideas and the computational algorithms, making students' learning of the algorithms meaningful rather than rote.

Using Patterns to Find Symbolic Algorithms for Fraction Arithmetic

To help students develop some conceptual basis for the algorithms for fraction arithmetic, have them use concrete materials or pictures to find answers to fraction arithmetic problems, then search for patterns showing how to manipulate the numerators and denominators of the given fractions to find the numerator and denominator of the answer. (They should keep all numbers in fraction form, not mixed numerals or whole numbers.)

Searching for patterns will help many students discover computational algorithms for fraction arithmetic. If students don't see the pattern at first, give them additional problems with answers. This will provide additional data for finding a pattern.

As you discuss the symbolic patterns as a class, it is critical that at some point you clearly describe and demonstrate the algorithms and give students opportunities to try them. In fact, be sure that each computational procedure that students discover is described verbally, algebraically, and with several numerical examples.

Addition and Subtraction Algorithms

Students should work on problems like those on **STUDENT SHEETS 45–47** to look for patterns to find algorithms for adding and subtracting fractions.

On Student Sheet 45, the two numbers to be added or subtracted have the same denominator. Ask questions to help students see the pattern. "To find the denominator of the sum or difference, use the common denominator. To find the numerator of the sum or difference, add or subtract the given numerators." For additional problems in which the added or subtracted fractions have a common denominator, you can give students problems such as 3/4 – 1/4, 7/8 – 5/8 and so on. Keep the sum a proper fraction. Be sure that students have graph paper that has at least as many rectangles in a row as the common denominator. As students work on the problems on this student sheet, probe for understanding with questions such as the following. "What do you do if you add or subtract fractions with a common denominator?" [To add or subtract two fractions that have a common denominator, add or subtract their numerators and put the result over their common denominator.] "Why is it okay to add or subtract the numerators if the fractions have a common denominator?" [Because you divided the whole into pieces of the same size.]

On Student Sheet 46, the denominator of one of the numbers to be added or subtracted is a multiple of the denominator of the other number. Ask questions to help students see the pattern. "What do we need to do before we can add or subtract these fractions?" [Get a common denominator.] "Why?" [So the fraction pieces are the same size.] "What is the common denominator?" [The larger of the two denominators.] "So what should we do?" [Convert the fraction with the smaller denominator into an equivalent fraction with the larger denominator. Then add or subtract as in fractions with a common denominator.] As additional problems in which the original fractions have a common denominator, you can give students problems such as 1/4 + 1/2, 3/4 – 3/12 and so on. Keep the sum a proper fraction. Be sure that students have graph paper that has at least as many rectangles in a row as the larger of the two given denominators.

On Student Sheet 47, the denominators are different and neither is a multiple of the other. Ask questions to help students see the pattern. "What do we need to do before we can add or subtract these fractions?" [Get a common denominator.] "Why?" [So the fraction pieces are the same size.] "What is a common denominator?" [The product of the two denominators.] "So what should we do?" [Convert the fractions to equivalent fractions with the common denominator. Then add or subtract as in fractions with a common denominator.] As additional problems in which the original fractions have a common denominator, you can give students problems such as 4/5 − 2/3, 2/5 + 1/4 and so on. Keep the sum a proper fraction. The number of squares that students should put in 1 should be the product of the denominators.

Ask students to describe the procedure they developed for problems on Student Sheet 47. For example, for addition, students might say, "To add fractions, change them to equivalent fractions with a common denominator, then add the numerators." *[What's the denominator for the answer?]* "It's the common denominator that you found."

Show students the symbolic algorithms that mathematicians use for adding and subtracting fractions.

$$\frac{a}{b} + \frac{c}{d} = \frac{ad}{bd} + \frac{bc}{bd} = \frac{ad + bc}{bd} \qquad \frac{a}{b} - \frac{c}{d} = \frac{ad}{bd} - \frac{bc}{bd} = \frac{ad - bc}{bd}$$

Then show them a couple of symbolically worked out examples: To find 2/31 + 4/5, you could use 31 × 5 = 155 as a common denominator and add: 10/155 + 124/155 = 134/155. To find 9/13 − 3/8, use 13 × 8 = 104 as the denominator and subtract: 72/104 − 39/104 = 33/104.

Multiplication

Students should solve problems like those on **STUDENT SHEET 48** 📥 to find a pattern that suggests a procedure for symbolically multiplying fractions. When students think they have found a pattern, have them describe it, keeping in mind that descriptions will differ among students, and that their descriptions often will require implementing the procedure on a specific example. For instance, a student might write and say the following to find 12/13 × 4/5:

Write: $\dfrac{12 \times 4}{13 \times 5} = \dfrac{48}{65}$.

Say: "*[Pointing]* Multiply the numerators for the numerator of the answer. Multiply the denominators for the denominator of the answer."

Show students correct notation for solving this problem:

$$\frac{12}{13} \times \frac{4}{5} = \frac{12 \times 4}{13 \times 5} = \frac{48}{65}$$

Explain that in algebra, we would describe this procedure with letters that stand for numbers.

$$\frac{a}{b} \times \frac{c}{d} = \frac{a \times c}{b \times d}$$

Then have students do additional examples on their own.

As students develop knowledge of the multiplication algorithm, probe with questions such as: "How is the numerator in the answer related to the numerators of the given fractions? How is the denominator in the answer related to the denominators of the given fractions?"

Division

Students should work on **STUDENT SHEET 49** ⬇ to look for a pattern that indicates how to symbolically divide fractions. Students should discover the following procedure, which again should be described verbally, with examples, and algebraically.

Verbal description: To divide two fractions, invert the second fraction, then multiply the inverted fraction by the first fraction.

For example, to find $\frac{3}{4} \div \frac{2}{7}$, *do the following*: $\frac{3}{4} \div \frac{2}{7} = \frac{3}{4} \times \frac{7}{2} = \frac{3 \times 7}{4 \times 2} = \frac{21}{8} = 2\frac{5}{8}$.

Explain that in algebra, we would describe this procedure with letters that stand for numbers.

$$\frac{a}{b} \div \frac{c}{d} = \frac{a}{b} \times \frac{d}{c} = \frac{a \times d}{b \times c}$$

As students develop knowledge of the division algorithm, probe with questions such as: "What procedure do you use to divide fractions? How do you know that this procedure works?" ["We did a bunch of problems with pictures, and we found a pattern."]

Finding Fractions of Large Whole Numbers

To foreshadow how instruction can help students understand arithmetic operations on fractions, instruction for students in Level 5 can deepen students' understanding of a procedure for using whole-number division and multiplication to find fractions of large numbers. Understanding this procedure is more cognitively accessible than understanding arithmetic operations on fractions.

In this instruction, we want to help students understand the following two-step procedure for finding a fraction of a whole number. To find *a/b* of *c*, first divide *c* by *b*, then multiply by *a* (we assume that *c* is divisible by *b*). For example, to find 3/4 of 100, we find 1/4 of 100 by dividing 100 by 4 (which gives 25), then we find 3/4 of 100 by multiplying 1/4 of 100 by 3 (which gives 75).

You can help students understand why this procedure works by having them connect pictorial and numeric actions step by step. For instance, to find 3/5 of 20, we can simultaneously ask students what steps to perform with pictures and with numbers.

What's the first step with pictures?	What's the first step with numbers? Why?
Divide 20 squares in 5 equal groups; count how many in each group?	$20 \div 5 = 4$ (4 is 1/5 of 20)
What's the second step with pictures?	What's the second step with numbers?
Shade and count the squares in 3 groups.	3 groups of $4 = 3 \times 4 = 12$ (12 is 3/5 of 20)

Ask questions to lead students through the same steps to find 3/5 of 50.

> Step 1: (Place-value picture) Divide 50 squares into 5 equal groups. How many in each group?
>
> (Numbers) $50 \div 5 = 10$ (10 is 1/5 of 50)

> Step 2: (Place-value picture) Shade and count the squares in 3 groups.
>
> (Numbers) $3 \times 10 = 30$ (30 is 3/5 of 50).

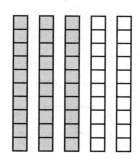

Students can practice this reasoning, and extend it to improper fractions, on **STUDENT SHEET 50**.

Teaching Students at Level 6: Moving to Solving Difficult Problems and Understanding Why Symbolic Fraction Computations Work

There are two major types of reasoning that must be deepened and refined for students to move to Level 7. First, students at this level have to significantly deepen their understanding of fractions and fraction arithmetic so that they can pictorially perform fraction arithmetic on difficult problems. Second, students have to understand more precisely and specifically the correspondence between computational and pictorial actions when performing fraction arithmetic. This requires students to analyze the sequence of actions they perform on physical or pictorial material to determine a corresponding set of arithmetic actions performed on numbers. This process, often called mathematical modeling, not only helps students learn about fractions but also helps them learn the critical mathematical practice of modeling.

Finding Equivalent Fractions

To help students understand numerical procedures for generating equivalent fractions, encourage them to connect multiplying the numerator and denominator of a fraction by the same number to subdividing or splitting fraction partitions. The example below shows the connection between this type of multiplication and splitting.

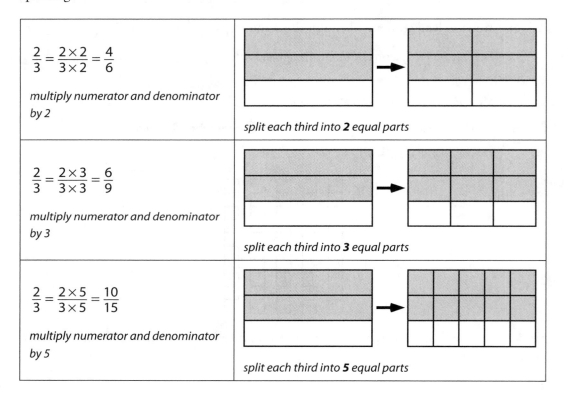

Ask questions that help students see, understand, and describe how actions on numbers and pictures correspond. *What patterns can you see in what we did? If the rectangle is partitioned into 3 thirds, and we split each third into 2 equal pieces, how many new equal pieces do we have in the whole rectangle?* [3 × 2 = 6] "In the shaded part of the rectangle? [2 × 2 = 4] What is the equivalent fraction we created by splitting thirds into 2 pieces? [4/6] What did we do with numbers to create 4/6 from 2/3?" [We multiplied both the numerator and denominator of 2/3 by 2.]

If the rectangle is partitioned into 3 thirds, and we split each third into 5 equal pieces, how many new equal pieces do we have in the whole rectangle? [3 × 5 = 15] *In the shaded part of the rectangle?* [2 × 5 = 10] *What is the equivalent fraction we created by splitting thirds into 5 pieces?* [10/15] *What did we do with numbers to create 10/15 from 2/3?* [We multiplied both the numerator and denominator of 2/3 by 5.]

Suppose I create a fraction equivalent to 2/3 by multiplying its numerator and denominator by 20. What equivalent fraction would I get? Explain what we have to do with this picture of 2/3 to find this same equivalent fraction.

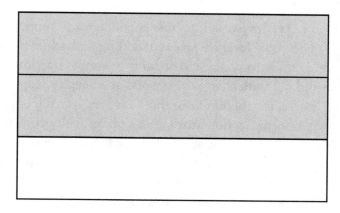

Help students consolidate their thinking by asking them to verbally describe their discovery about generating equivalent fractions: "You can find a fraction that is equivalent to a given fraction by multiplying the numerator and denominator of the given fraction by the same number. How is that numerical procedure related to drawing pictures?" *[If you multiply the numerator and denominator by 20, you have to divide the original fraction pieces each into 20 equal pieces.]*

Encourage students to see how their reasoning can be expressed algebraically by saying, "In algebra, we would describe the procedure we discovered for finding equivalent fractions as follows:"

$$\frac{a}{b} = \frac{a \times m}{b \times m}$$

For example:

$$\frac{6}{9} = \frac{6 \times 4}{9 \times 4} = \frac{24}{36}$$

You can use the same pictures as above but "reverse" the splitting process by combining subdivisions within partitions to help students see that we can also create equivalent fractions by dividing the numerator and denominator of the given fraction by the same number.

$$\frac{a}{b} = \frac{a \div n}{b \div n}$$

For example:

$$\frac{6}{9} = \frac{6 \div 3}{9 \div 3} = \frac{2}{3}$$

Have students use **STUDENT SHEET 51** 📥 to further investigate the connection between these pictorial and numeric actions for finding equivalent fractions.

Solving Difficult Addition and Subtraction Problems Visually: Understanding the Process

To move students to Level 7, instruction must encourage and support them in understanding at a deep conceptual level *the process* of adding and subtracting fractions pictorially. At Level 5, students could find answers to simple fraction arithmetic problems, but they did not understand the process at a deep conceptual level. To move students to Level 7, instruction must focus on conceptually understanding the processes needed to perform fraction arithmetic with difficult problems. Note that because Level 7 is so hard to achieve, and so few students achieve it, it is productive and meaningful for instruction to teach the symbolic fraction arithmetic algorithms once students have achieved Level 5. Instruction can then return to deepen students' understanding of the processes and how to use them to justify algorithms once students have reached Level 6.

As an example, tell students that we want to do the addition problem 2/3 + 1/4. The picture below shows 2/3 and 1/4 represented with identical squares.

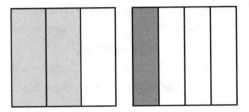

Ask students, "To add or subtract 2/3 and 1/4 pictorially, what is the first thing we must do?" [We must find fractions equivalent to 2/3 and 1/4 with pieces that are the same size.] "How do we get pieces the same size?" [We get the pieces the same size by creating equivalent fractions with a common denominator.] "What is a common denominator for thirds and fourths? [12] How do we know what a common denominator is?" [It's the product of the original denominators, 3 and 4.] "Okay, so in the picture below, if we use the common denominator of 12, we get pieces of the same size—twelfths."

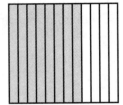 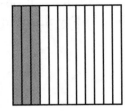

Continue the discussion with students: "Once we get the pieces the same size, we add or subtract the numerators and put the result over the common denominator."

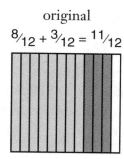
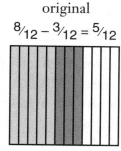

original
$^8/_{12} + {}^3/_{12} = {}^{11}/_{12}$

original
$^8/_{12} - {}^3/_{12} = {}^5/_{12}$

Students can further develop their knowledge of this process and reasoning by working problems using grid paper. They can make the whole contain a number of rectangles equal to a common denominator for the two fractions, then represent each of the given fractions as equivalent fractions with the common denominator before representing the sum or difference. For example, with grid paper, we might represent the problem 2/3 + 1/4 as follows:

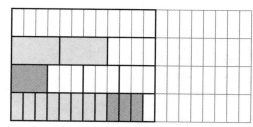

1

$^2/_3$

$^1/_4$

$^2/_3 + {}^1/_4 = {}^8/_{12} + {}^3/_{12} = {}^{11}/_{12}$

Remember, the goal of these activities is for students to develop a deeper understanding and conceptualization of the pictorial procedures for adding and subtracting fractions, not merely to learn more procedures. So, while doing these activities, ask questions that get students to focus on and understand the process: "How do we add and subtract fractions? What do we do, and why?" [We convert the given fractions to equivalent fractions with a common denominator, then add or subtract these fractions.] "Why do we get a common denominator?" [To determine what fraction a picture depicts, the pieces must be the same size.] "How do we find a common denominator?" [We multiply the two given denominators together.] "Why is the product of the original fraction denominators a common denominator?" [Because the product of the denominators can be evenly divided by both denominators, which means that there are numbers that can be used to multiply the numerator and denominator of the original fractions to get equivalent fractions with a common denominator. The least common multiple of the original denominators also has this property.]

Have students do the following problems using graph paper, then check their answers with the addition or subtraction algorithms. Ask questions to probe and encourage student understanding: "Describe how you did the problem on graph paper. How many squares did you use for 1? How did you know to use this number for 1? What is the common denominator? Why does this number work as a common denominator?"

        2/5 + 1/4
        2/5 – 1/4
        3/4 – 2/3
        3/4 + 2/3

Solving Difficult Multiplication Problems Visually: Why Multiply the Numerators and the Denominators?

Have students use graph paper to solve problems like those on **STUDENT SHEET 52** ⬇ to help them make sense of the procedure for multiplying fractions: The product of two fractions has the product of the numerators as its numerator and the product of the denominators as its denominator.

$$\frac{a}{b} \times \frac{c}{d} = \frac{a \times c}{b \times d}$$

Before students start their individual work on Student Sheet 52, lead a discussion of Problem 1 (2/3 × 4/5) as follows: Draw a rectangle having 3 rows and 5 columns to represent 1. *Why should we use this size rectangle?* [We want to be able to divide the rectangle into thirds horizontally and fifths vertically.] *Now make 4/5 using columns and 2/3 using rows.*

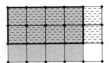

"What does the inside of the double-shaded rectangle (smaller dark rectangle) represent?" [2/3 of 4/5, or 4/5 of 2/3] "How many squares are in the double-shaded region?" [2 × 4] "Where did the 2 and 4 come from in the symbols and in the picture?" [2 and 4 are the numerators in the original fractions. In the picture, 2 is the number of shaded rows for 2/3, and 4 is the number of shaded columns for 4/5.] "What fraction of the whole rectangle is each square? [15] Where did the 15 come from?" [The original rectangle has 15 total squares in it because there are 3 total rows for 2/3 and 5 total columns for 4/5; 3 and 5 are the original denominators.] "What fraction of the whole is double shaded?" [8/15] Be sure to write the problem symbolically. "So we have found that:"

$$\frac{2}{3} \times \frac{4}{5} = \frac{2 \times 4}{3 \times 5} = \frac{8}{15}$$

Solving Difficult Division Problems Visually: Why Invert and Multiply?

Recall the "invert and multiply" procedure for dividing fractions: $\frac{a}{b} \div \frac{c}{d} = \frac{a}{b} \times \frac{d}{c}$. A more precise description of this procedure is: To divide one fraction by a second fraction, multiply the first fraction by the reciprocal of the second fraction.

Using pictures to understand why the invert and multiply division algorithm works is difficult. So you should demonstrate this idea with some well-chosen examples, asking probing questions throughout the discussion. Do this kind of demonstration a couple of times, then give students problems to try on their own, then have a class discussion of student work. Here is a sample discussion that you might have with students to find 5 ÷ 3/4.

"We want to use pictures to understand why we solve the problem 5 ÷ 3/4 by inverting and multiplying: 5 ÷ 3/4 = 5 × 4/3. What are we trying to find when we solve 5 ÷ 3/4?" [How many times 3/4 goes into 5, or how many copies of 3/4 are in 5.] "To think about this problem, it is helpful to first think about an easier problem: How many copies of 3/4 are in 1? Look at the picture below that shows 1, 3/4, and 1 1/3 copies of 3/4."

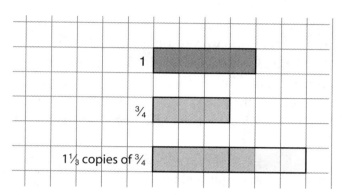

Ask students, "How many 3/4s are in 1?" The answer, 1 1/3, is difficult for most students to comprehend. Many students think the answer is 1 1/4 because each square is 1/4 of the original whole or 1. So ask the question several different, but equivalent ways: "How many copies of 3/4 are in 1?" [One whole copy and 1/3 of another copy.] The important thing for students to understand here is that 1 square is 1/3 of a copy of 3/4, not 1/3 of the original 1. Another way to rephrase the question is: "If 3/4 is the measuring unit, what does 1 measure? Think about yards, with 3/4 playing the role of a yard stick. If the thing I want to measure in yards is the top bar (the original 1, which is 4 feet long), how many yards long is it?" [It's 1 1/3 yards.]

"How does knowing that there are 1 1/3 copies of 3/4 in 1 help us figure out how many 3/4s are in 5?" [There are 5 ones in 5.] "How does that help us?" [There are 1 1/3 copies of 3/4 in each of the ones in 5.] Help students see this with the picture below.

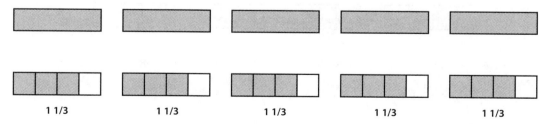

1 1/3   1 1/3   1 1/3   1 1/3   1 1/3

Ask, "So how many 3/4s are in 5?"
[Because there are 1 1/3 copies of 3/4 in each 1, there are 5 times 1 1/3 copies of 3/4 in 5.] "So I can write what you just said as: 5 ÷ 3/4 = 5 × 1 1/3."

"What happens when we write 1 1/3 in this equation as an improper fraction?" [We get 5 ÷ 3/4 = 5 × 4/3].

"So what does this equation tell us?" [That we find the answer to the division problem by inverting the divisor and multiplying by it.]

We can use numbers and symbols to summarize all the work we have just done as follows:

1) $5 \div 3/4 = (1 + 1 + 1 + 1 + 1) \div 3/4$

2) $ = (1 \div 3/4) + (1 \div 3/4) + (1 \div 3/4) + (1 \div 3/4) + (1 \div 3/4)$

3) $ = 1\ 1/3 + 1\ 1/3 + 1\ 1/3 + 1\ 1/3 + 1\ 1/3$

4) $ = 4/3 + 4/3 + 4/3 + 4/3 + 4/3$

5) $ = 5 \times 4/3$

Ask questions to probe and encourage students' understanding of each step in the symbolic representation. "How do we know that Line 1 is true?" [5 = 1 + 1 + 1 + 1 + 1] "How do we know that Line 2 is true?" [the distributive property] "How do we know that Line 3 is true?" [We showed that in our two pictures.] "How do we know that Line 4 is true?" [because the mixed number 1 1/3 equals the improper fraction 4/3] "How do we know that Line 5 is true?" [adding 4/3 five times is like multiplying 5 times 4/3]

Use Student Sheet 53 to give students additional experiences showing how division of fractions can be accomplished by the invert and multiply procedure. If students are having difficulty, give them some additional guidance. For example, for Problem 1, show the picture below and ask, "If the top bar shows 1, what is the gray part in the bottom bar? [2/3] How many copies of 2/3 fit in 1?" [1 1/2]

Then show the picture below and ask, "How many copies of 2/3 fit in 4?"

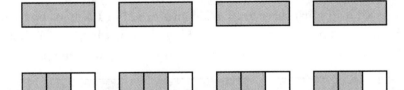

The above picture shows that the number of copies of 2/3 in 4 is:

$$1\frac{1}{2} + 1\frac{1}{2} + 1\frac{1}{2} + 1\frac{1}{2} = 4 \times 1\frac{1}{2} = 6.$$

So $4 \div \dfrac{2}{3} = 4 \times \dfrac{3}{2}$.

Note that another way to see that 6 copies of 2/3 fit in 4 is with the picture below. However, this picture does not help explain the invert and multiply procedure.

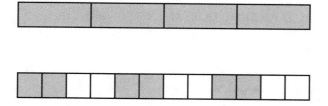

After discussing Problem 1 as a class, have students continue with the other problems on Student Sheet 53.

Appendix

CBA Assessment Tasks for Fractions

These problems can be used in individual interviews with children or in class as instructional activities. However, no matter which use you choose, it is critical to get the students to write and describe or discuss their strategies. Only then can you use the CBA levels to interpret students' responses and decide on needed instruction.

Guide for Interviewing Students with CBA Tasks

The purpose of interviewing students with CBA tasks is to determine how they are reasoning and, more specifically, to determine what CBA levels of reasoning students are using for the tasks. Before the interview, CBA teachers said the following to students:

> I am going to give you some problems. I would like to know what you think while you solve these problems. So, tell me everything you think as you do the problems. Try to think out loud. Tell me what you are doing and why you are doing it. I will also ask you questions to help me understand what you are thinking. For instance, if you say something that I don't understand, I will ask you questions about it.

If you don't understand what a student is saying, you could ask, "I don't understand, could you explain that again?" or "What do you mean by such-and-such?" Try to get students to explain in their own words rather than paraphrasing what you think they mean and asking if they agree. If, during an interview, a student asked whether his or her answers are correct, we told the student that for this interview it does not really matter. We are interested in what he or she thinks.

Students responded to our request to "think out loud" in two ways. Many students were quite capable of thinking out loud as they solved problems. They told us what they were thinking and doing as they thought and did it. Other students, however, seemed unable to think aloud as they completed problems. They worked in silence, but then gave us detailed accounts of what they did *after* they finished doing it.

The following tasks cover a large range of reasoning about fractions. You probably will not want to give all the problems to your students, at least not at one time. For students in Grades 1–4, problems 1–12 are suggested, based on grade level and curriculum. Problems 13–17 are more appropriate for Grades 4–6. Of course, you can alter these suggestions based on your curriculum. Many of the problems have notes indicating particular aspects of students' reasoning that are emphasized by the problems.

Additional assessment tasks (including more tasks appropriate for Grades 4–5) may be downloaded from this book's website, www.heinemann.com/products/E04345.aspx.

1. Three people want to share 12 cookies equally. Show and tell how many cookies each person should get.

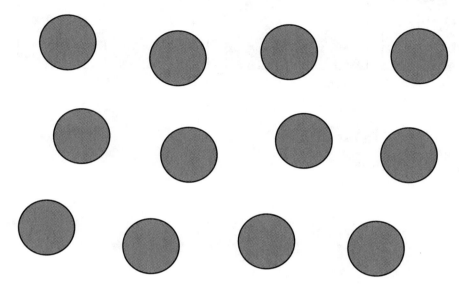

2. Four people want to share 2 cakes equally. Show how much each person should get.

3. a. Circle the figures below that show one-half. Explain your answers.

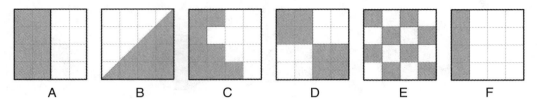

A   B   C   D   E   F

b. Which figure has the larger shaded part, Figure A or Figure B, or are they the same? Explain your answer.

4. Circle the pictures below that show 3/4. Explain your answers.

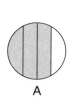 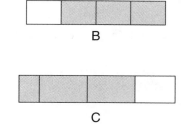 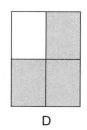 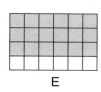

5. Shade 2/5 of the inside of the black rectangle.

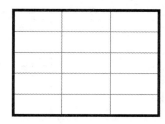

6. Which fraction is larger, 2/3 or 2/5, or are they the same? Explain with pictures or words.

7. Tell what fraction of the large square is shaded. Explain your answer.

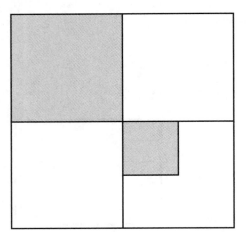

8. Explain how you found your answers.

Shade 1/4 of the circles.

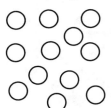

Shade 2/3 of the circles.

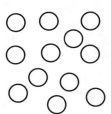

9. Draw a picture to show 4/3. Explain your answer.

Name _____   Date _____

10. Find the following. Explain your answers.

2/3 of 15 = _____

5/4 of 20 = _____

11.

1/4 of a cake is shown at the right.

Draw what the whole cake looks like.

Explain your answer.

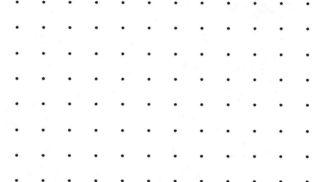

2/3 of a cake is shown at the right.

Draw what the whole cake looks like.

Explain your answer.

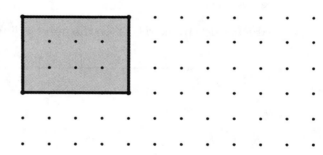

12. Jon ate 12 cookies. That was 3/4 of the whole bag of cookies. How many cookies were in the whole bag? Explain your answer.

13. Name the fraction marked by X on the number line. Explain your answer.

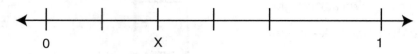

14. Name the fraction marked by X on the number line. Explain your answer.

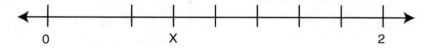

Name _____   Date _____

15. Find the following. Explain your answer.

3/4 of 840 = _____

16.

Asked to find 1/2 + 1/3, Harry drew the picture at the right and said, "1 of 2 parts, plus 1 of 3 parts equals 2 of 5 parts. So the answer is 2/5."

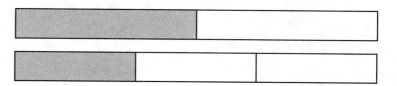

Tell whether Harry's reasoning is correct or incorrect and explain why.

17. Draw rectangles on the dot paper to show how to solve the problems. Give the answer to each problem and explain why your picture shows that answer. If you can, show how to solve the problem symbolically.

1/2 + 1/5

1/2 − 1/3

1/2 × 1/4

1/2 ÷ 1/3

2 ÷ 5

CBA Levels for Each Task

The descriptions below show sample student responses at various levels of sophistication.

PROBLEM 1

Three people want to share 12 cookies equally. Show and tell how many cookies each person should get.

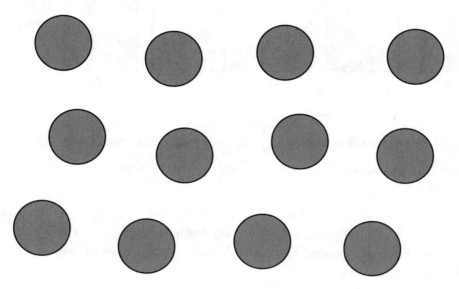

Level 0.1: Student gives a different number of cookies to each person, or does not partition all the cookies.

Level 0.2: Student gives 4 cookies to each person.

Levels 1–7: Not applicable.

PROBLEM 2

Four people want to share 2 cakes equally. Show how much each person should get.

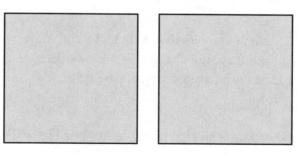

Level 0.1: Student gives a different amount of cake to each person, or does not partition all the cake.

Level 0.2: Student's drawing shows that each person gets 1/2 a cake (but student does not know that the portion that each person gets is called one-half).

Levels 1–7: Not applicable.

PROBLEM 3

a. Circle the figures below that show one-half. Explain your answers.

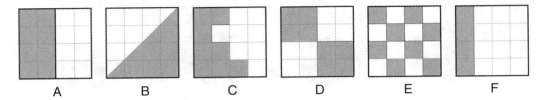

A   B   C   D   E   F

Levels 0.1–0.2: Not applicable.

Level 1: Student says that only A and/or B look like a half.

Level 2: Student says that A, B, and perhaps F are halves because in each one part is shaded and one part is not.

Level 3: Student answers that A–E are each one-half and explains his reasoning as follows: A is one-half because there are 2 equal pieces and 1 is shaded. Same thing for B. On C, you just move this shaded part here over to here so they look the same (see arrow).

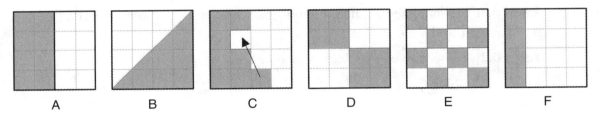

A   B   C   D   E   F

On D, move the bottom shaded square to the left, under the top shaded square. On E, you can move all the shaded squares to the left. F is not one half because the parts aren't the same.

Levels 4.1–4.2: Student answers that A, B, C, D, and E are one-half because 8 squares are shaded and 8 are not shaded. [Might say that you can tell A and B are one-half because they both have two equal parts.]

Levels 5–7: Not applicable.

b. Which figure has the larger shaded part, Figure A or Figure B, or are they the same? Explain your answer.

Levels 0.1–1: Student says that the shaded part of B (or A) is larger because it just looks bigger. Or student says that the shaded part of B is larger because it is just as tall as the shaded part in A but it is wider.

Level 2: Student might say that the shaded parts are equal because each is half. Asked why, the student says that the shaded parts are equal because each square is divided into two parts. But the student might also say that the shaded part in B looks bigger. No firm justification is possible.

Level 3: Student says that the shaded parts are equal because each is half of the same square. Asked why, the student says that the shaded parts are equal because you can cut the left triangular part of B off and turn it up on top to make A (see figure below). So the student justification is based on correct visual reasoning, not logical deduction.

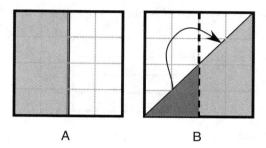

A   B

Levels 4.1–4.2: Student says that the shaded parts are equal because each is half of the square and the squares are equal. Student might also justify this conclusion by saying that each shaded part contains 8 squares (in counting the squares in B, the student pieces halves along the diagonal together). Or the student says that because you are dividing both Squares A and B into equal parts, and that there are 16 squares total in each square, the shaded parts each have 16 ÷ 2 = 8 squares in them.

Levels 5–7: Not applicable. *[Taking half of 16 can be thought of as multiplying a fraction 1/2 times a whole number 16. However, in CBA we first consider taking half of 16 in terms of finding a fractional part of a set of objects.]*

PROBLEM 4

Circle the pictures below that show 3/4. Explain your answers.

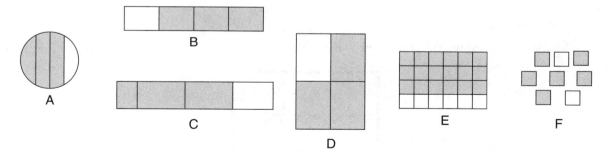

Level 0: Student doesn't understand what the problem is asking. So answers would be random.

Level 1: Student may say that A–D are or are not 3/4 depending on what kinds of visual examples he or she can recall for 3/4. A and C are just as likely to be selected as 3/4 as B and D. However, student says that E and F are not examples of 3/4. For example, for E, student says that there's too many pieces to be fourths.

Level 2: Student says that Shapes A–D are 3/4 because they all have 4 parts and 3 are shaded. Shapes E and F are not 3/4 because they have too many pieces.

Level 3: Student says that B and D are 3/4 because they both have 4 equal parts and 3 are shaded; A and C are not 3/4 because their parts aren't equal. E is 3/4 because you can divide it so that 3 of 4 equal parts are shaded (draws on figure as shown below). Student says that F is not 3/4 because 6 squares are shaded.

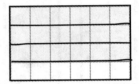

Levels 4.1–4.2: Student's reasons about Shapes A–D are the same as in Level 3. For Shape E, student draws on the picture the same as in Level 3 above, but talks about squares: "Each row has 6 squares, so the rows are equal; and 3 of the 4 rows are shaded, so that's 3/4." Student identifies F as being 3/4 shaded because there are 3 groups of 2 squares shaded, and 1 group of 2 squares unshaded (see below).

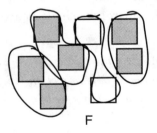

F

Levels 5–7: Not applicable.

PROBLEM 5

Shade 2/5 of the inside of the black rectangle.

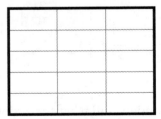

Levels 0–1: Student shades 2, 5, or 2 and 5 small rectangles.

Cognition-Based Assessment and Teaching of Fractions

Level 2: Student says that you are supposed to shade 2 out of 5 parts. So the student first makes a section of 5 small rectangles, then shades 2 of them.

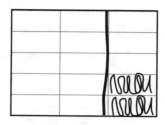

Level 3: Student says that each row is one-fifth, so you have to shade two rows.

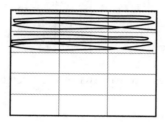

Levels 4.1–4.2: Student says that each row is one-fifth and there are 3 little rectangles in a row. So 2/5 is 6 little rectangles. Student says that you can shade any 6 rectangles.

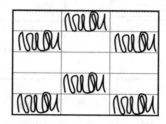

Level 5: Student says that there are 15 small rectangles in the large black-outline rectangle. To find 2/5 of 15, divide 15 into 5 equal groups, which gives 3 in each group. Then 2/5 is 2 groups of 3, equals 6. So color any 6 of the small rectangles.

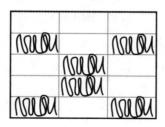

Levels 6–7: Not applicable.

PROBLEM 6

Which fraction is larger, 2/3 or 2/5, or are they the same? Explain with pictures or words.

Levels 0–1: Student says that 2/5 is bigger because 5 is bigger than 3.

Level 2: Student draws 2/3 and 2/5 without keeping the whole constant and concludes that these fractions are the same.

Levels 3–4.1: Student says, after drawing pictures for 2/3 and 2/5, that 2/3 is bigger.

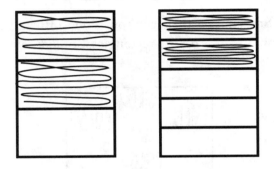

Level 4.2: Student says that 2/3 is bigger because the numerators are the same, and thirds are bigger than fifths, so 2 thirds must be bigger than 2 fifths.

Level 5: Student converts both 2/3 and 2/5 to equivalent fractions with a common denominator of 15. The student divides each one in the 2 and 3 of 2/3 into 5 equal parts and to get 10/15. The student divides each one in the 2 and 5 of 2/5 into 3 equal parts to get 6/15. Because 10/15 is bigger than 6/15, the student concludes that 2/3 is bigger than 2/5.

Levels 6–7: Not applicable.

PROBLEM 7

Tell what fraction of the large square is shaded. Explain your answer.

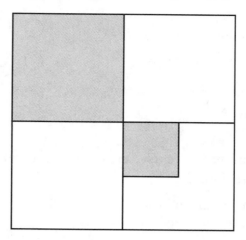

Level 0: Student simply counts the 2 shaded parts.

Level 1: Student focuses on the large shaded square as it fits in the whole figure and says 1/4.

Level 2: Student counts shaded pieces, then counts the total pieces and says that 2/5 is shaded.

Level 3: Student says that there are 4 little shaded squares in the big shaded square, so 1¼ is shaded.

Levels 4.1–4.2: Student says you can tell that there are 16 little squares in the shape and 5 are shaded. So 5/16 is shaded. Or student draws the picture below and says 5/16.

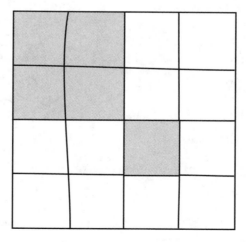

Level 5: Student says that the big shaded square is 1/4. The small shaded square is 1/4 of 1/4, which is 1/16 of the whole. Because you can see that the big shaded square, which is 1/4, is also 4/16, the shaded part is 4/16 plus 1/16, which is 5/16.

Levels 6–7: Not applicable.

PROBLEM 8

Shade 1/4 of the circles.

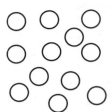

Shade 2/3 of the circles.

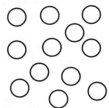

Levels 0–1: Student shades 1 circle (and possibly 4 more) for 1/4, and 2 circles (and possibly 3 more) for 2/3.

Level 2: Student draws the following:

[For1/4]

[For 2/3]

[Teacher: How many circles did you shade?]

Student: *I don't know.*

OR

Student: [For 1/4] *I did 1 out of 4.*

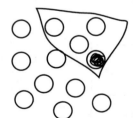

Student: [For 2/3] *2 out of 3.*

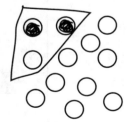

Level 3: Student draws and says the following:

Student: *I kept doing one-fourths.*

Student: *I kept doing two-thirds.*

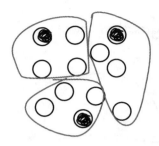 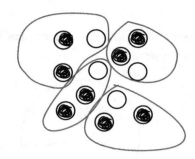

Level 4.1: Student says the following:

[For 1/4] Make 4 equal parts [loops 4 groups of 3 circles]. Shade one part. So the answer is 3.

[For 2/3] Make 3 groups, shade 2 groups. So the answer is 8.

Note that students must reach Level 4 before they can correctly answer the question, "How many circles must be shaded to make 1/4 or 2/3 of the circles?"

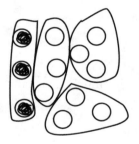 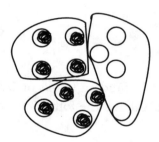

Levels 4.2–5: Student says the following:

[For 1/4] There are 4 threes in 12, so 1/4 of 12 is 3.

[For 2/3] 1/3 of 12 would be 4, so 2/3 of 12 is 8.

If the student seems to know a numerical procedure for solving these problems, ask why the procedure works.

If the student understands why the procedure works, then he or she is reasoning at Level 4. Otherwise, the reasoning level is lower.

Levels 6–7: Not applicable.

PROBLEM 9

Draw a picture to show 4/3. Explain your answer.

Level 0: Student draws 4 circles then 3 circles.

Level 1: Student draws a circle divided into 3 parts, then one of those sections into 4 parts.

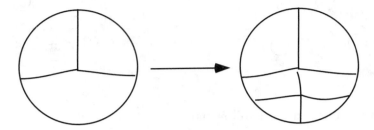

Level 2: Student draws 3/4 instead of 4/3 because the student thinks fractions must always be portions of one whole.

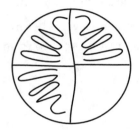

Level 3: Student thinks of 4/3 via the process of iterating 1/3, visually. So student draws the following for 4/3.

Levels 4–5: Student draws and shades a whole divided into 3 equal parts and another identical whole divided into 3 equals parts and shades 1 part. Asked what he or she did, student says, "One whole is 3 thirds, and one more third makes 4/3."

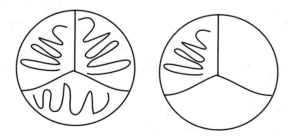

Levels 6–7: Not applicable.

Cognition-Based Assessment and Teaching of Fractions

PROBLEM 10

Find the following. Explain your answers.

	2/3 of 15 = _____	5/4 of 20 = _____
Level 0	Student says 2 + 3 + 15 is 20.	Student says 5 + 4 + 20 equals 29.
Level 1	Student draws 2/3.  	Student: *[After drawing the picture below]* I drew 5 groups of 4. That's 20. 
Level 2	Student draws 15 copies of a 2/3-shaded circle. The student then counts each shaded piece, getting 30. 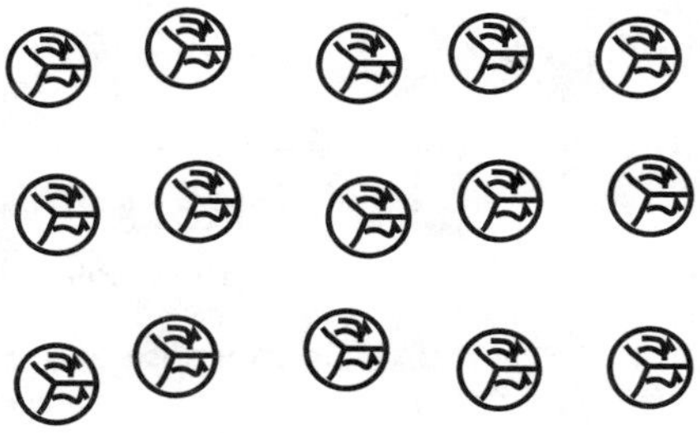 	Student draws 20 circles. The student then shades 5, then 4 more, then counts 9 shaded circles. 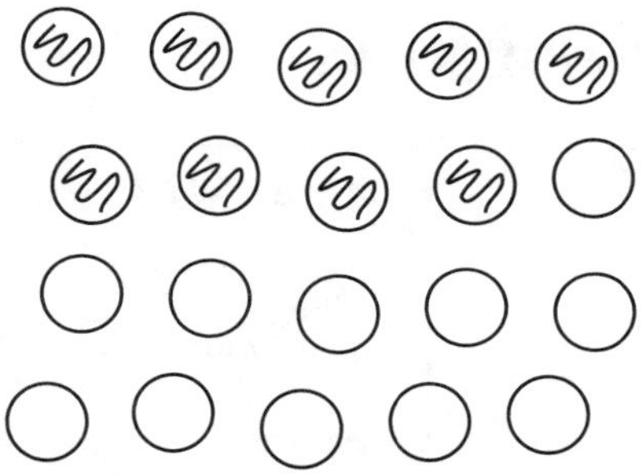
Level 3	Student draws 15 circles, then uses 3 for a representation of 2/3. 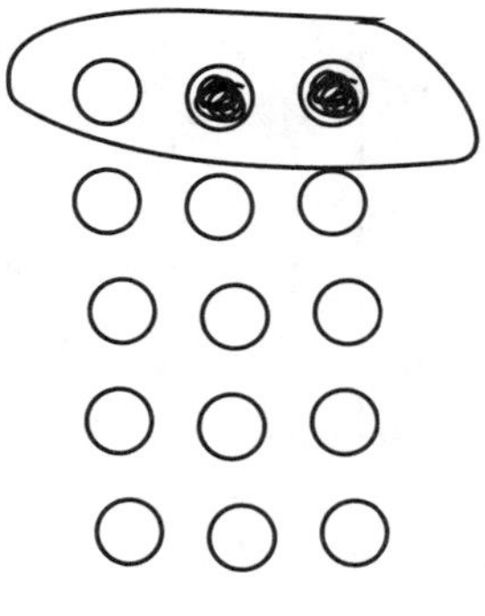 	Student draws 20 circles, then shades 1/4 on 5 of them and counts the 5 shaded parts for an answer of 5. 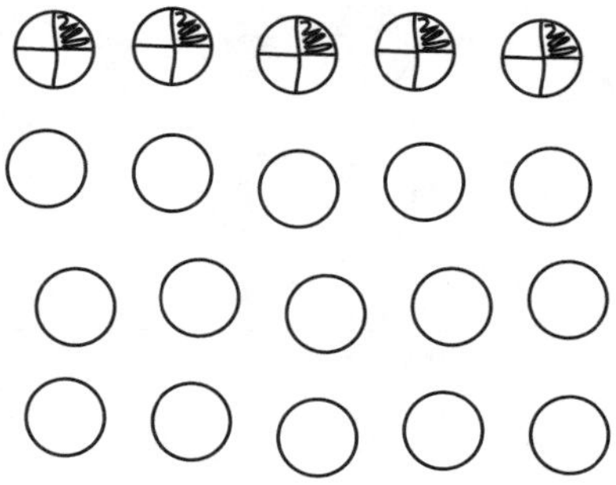

	2/3 of 15 = _____	5/4 of 20 = _____
Level 4.1	Student draws the following, saying that he or she needs to divide 15 into 3 equal groups and take 2 of them. That gives 10. 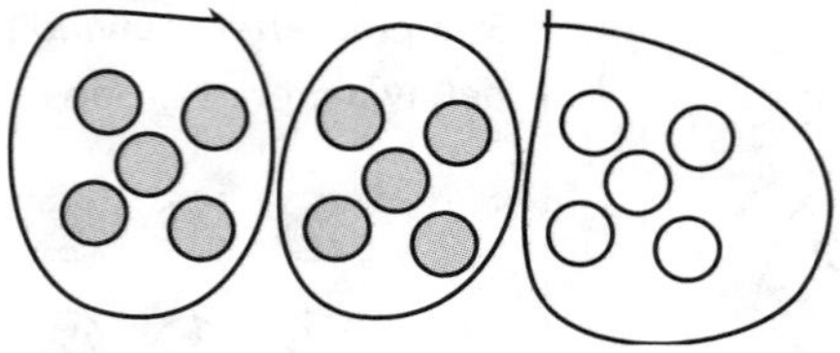	Student: [After drawing the picture below] 20 is the whole, and fourths mean 4 equal groups. There are 4 groups in the whole, and one more group, so that's 5, 10, 15, 20, 25. 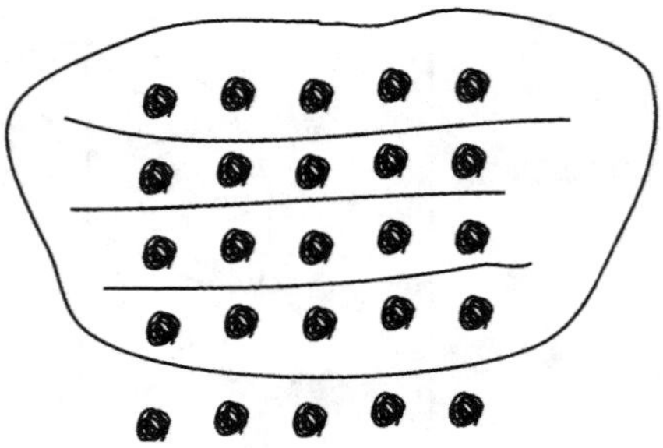
Level 4.2	Student says that 15 divided into 3 equal groups is 5 in each group, times 2 equals 10.	Student says that 20 divided into 4 equal groups is 5 in each group, times 5 equals 25.
Levels 5–7	Not applicable.	Not applicable.

PROBLEM 11

	1/4 of a cake is shown. Draw what the whole cake looks like. Explain your answer. 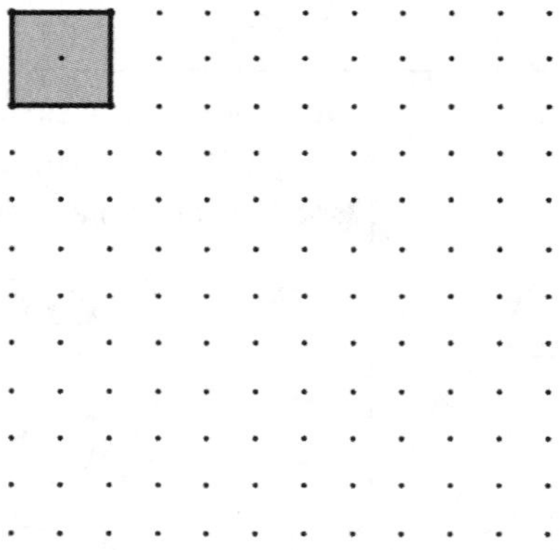 	2/3 of a cake is shown. Draw what the whole cake looks like. Explain your answer. 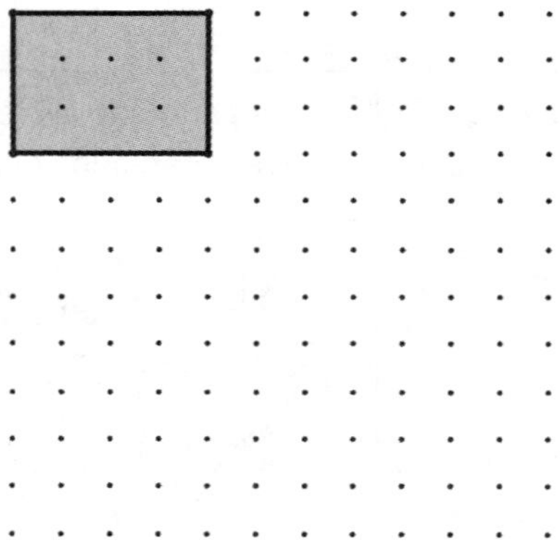

Levels 0–1	Not applicable.	Not applicable.
Level 2	Student says that you have to divide the pieces up and count 1 out of 4 pieces.	Student says that you have to divide the pieces up and count 2 out of 3 pieces.
Level 3	Student says it's fourths, so you have to make 4 parts.	Student says that because it's thirds, you make 3 parts. OR You make 3 parts and shade 2.
Level 4.1	Student says it's fourths, so you have to make 4 parts.	Student says that you have to divide the shaded part into 2 equal parts and that each of these parts is a third. You need 3 thirds for the whole.

Level 4.2	Student reasons that if 4 squares is 1/4, then 16 squares is the whole. So the cake has 16 squares.	Student reasons that if 12 squares is 2/3, then 12 squares is 2 groups. So 1 group, which is 1/3, is 6 squares. So the whole cake would be 3 groups of 6, equals 18 squares.
Levels 5–7	Not applicable.	Not applicable.

PROBLEM 12

	Jon ate 12 cookies. That was 3/4 of the whole bag of cookies. How many cookies were in the whole bag? Explain your answer.
Levels 0–1	Not applicable.
Level 2	Student draws a picture of 3/4 of one cookie.
Level 3	Student draws 12 cookies. The student then circles 4 of the cookies and shades 3 to make 3/4. The student says there are 4 cookies. Or student shades 3/4 of each of 12 cookies, but cannot determine how many are shaded.

Level 4.1	Student draws 12 circles. She says that because 12 is 3/4, it's 3 groups, and she circles 3 groups of 4 circles. She then shades these circles and says that there has to be another group of 4, which she draws. She then circles all the circles and counts them: 4, 8, 12, 16.
	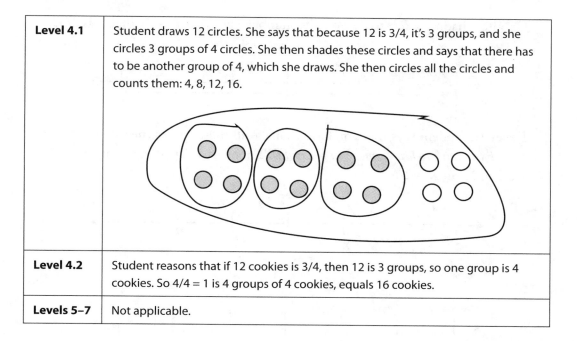
Level 4.2	Student reasons that if 12 cookies is 3/4, then 12 is 3 groups, so one group is 4 cookies. So 4/4 = 1 is 4 groups of 4 cookies, equals 16 cookies.
Levels 5–7	Not applicable.

PROBLEM 13

Name the fraction marked by X on the number line. Explain your answer.

Levels 0–1: Not applicable.

Level 2: After counting and numbering all hash marks, student says that 1 is at 6, and X is at 3, so X is 3/6.

Or student counts spaces between hash marks as shown below, getting 2/5.

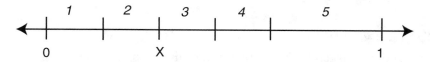

Or, after shading a rectangle over the number line, student says that X is 2/5.

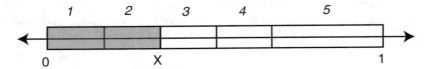

Level 3: Student says that you have to make all these spaces the same size first *[adds hash mark to last segment on the right]*. There are 6 equal segments in 1; there are 2 in X. So X is 2/6.

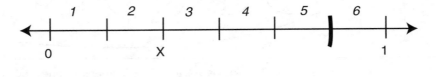

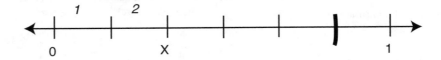

Or student says that all these spaces have to be the same size; so 2 in the beginning equal 1 at the end. So there are 3 equal spaces like this *[drawing]*, and X is at the first one. So X is 1/3.

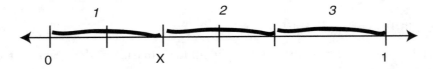

Levels 4.1–4.2: Student says the same as in Level 3 but now understands X as being at a location, instead of marking off three equal segments of size 1/3. (In Level 3, students get the right answer because of the procedure they apply; in Level 4, students understand points on the number line marking off directed distances.)

Levels 5–7: Not applicable.

PROBLEM 14

Name the fraction marked by X on the number line. Explain your answer.

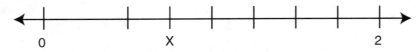

Level 0: Not applicable.

Level 1: Student says that X looks like a third.

Cognition-Based Assessment and Teaching of Fractions

Level 2: After counting and numbering all hash marks, student says that there are 8 marks and X is at 3, so X is 3/8.

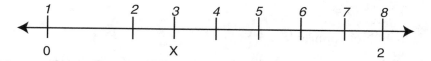

Or, after drawing a shaded rectangle over the number line, student says that X is 2/7.

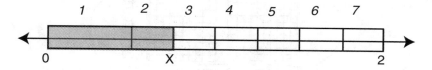

Or, imagining this same kind of shaded rectangle reasoning, student might count spaces between hash marks as shown below, still getting 2/7.

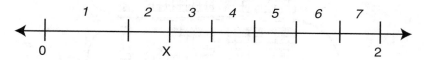

Level 3: Student says that you have to make all these spaces the same size first *[adds hash mark to first segment on the left]*. There are 8 equal segments; there are 3 in X. So X is 3/8.

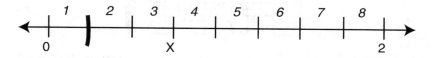

Levels 4.1–4.2: Student says that you have to make all these spaces the same size first *[adds hash mark to first segment on the left]*. There are 8 equal segments in 2, so there must be 4 segments in 1 *[marks 1 on the number line]*. So X is at 3/4.

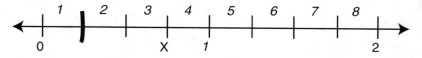

Levels 5–7: Not applicable.

PROBLEM 15

Find the following. Explain your answer.

3/4 of 840 = _____

Levels 0–4: Not applicable.

Level 5 Student uses base-ten blocks to represent 840, divides it into 4 equal groups of 210, then combines three of these groups to get 630.

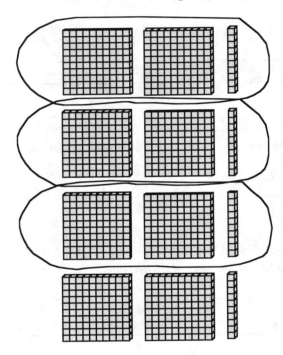

Level 6–7: Student divides 840 by 4, getting 210. The student then multiplies 210 by 3 to get his or her answer of 630. The student could give the Level 5 explanation if asked.

PROBLEM 16

Asked to find 1/2 + 1/3, Harry drew the picture below and said, "1 of 2 parts, plus 1 of 3 parts = 2 of 5 parts. So the answer is 2/5."

Tell whether Harry's reasoning is correct or incorrect and explain why.

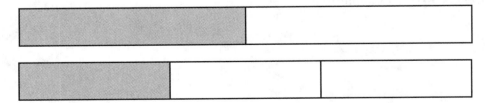

Levels 0–1: Not applicable.

Level 2: Student: "It's right. He counted 2 shaded pieces out of 5 pieces altogether."

Level 3: Student: "It's wrong. The pieces are not the same, so they can't be fifths."

Level 4: Student says that Harry is wrong because he does not have equal pieces and he uses 2 wholes when counting pieces.

Level 5: Student says to first get a common denominator, sixths. So *[writing]* it's 3/6 + 2/6 = 5/6, which is not 2/5. Student then shows how to do the problem pictorially.

> **Student:** "First, you have to cut up the wholes into sixths" *[draws as shown below].*

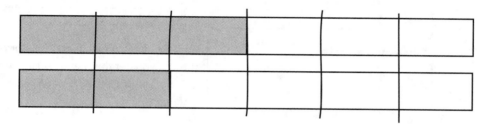

> **Student:** "Then take these 2 on the bottom from 1/3 and put them up here with the 1/2 *[crosses out 2 shaded sixths from 1/3 and shades in 2 additional sixths in the 1/2 picture].* So it's 5/6."

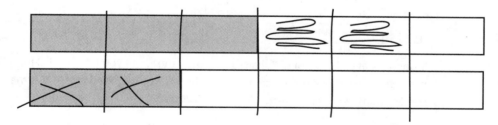

Level 6–7: Student says that 1/2 + 1/3 = 3/6 + 2/6 = 5/6. If asked why this solution is correct, the student can draw a picture to illustrate as in Level 5.

PROBLEM 17

Note. Level 6 and Level 7 reasoning on Problem 17 can be distinguished by asking appropriate follow-up questions of students who give initial answers that appear to be at Level 6.

Draw rectangles on the dot paper to show how to solve the problems. Give the answer to each problem and explain why your picture shows that answer. If you can, show how to solve the problem symbolically.

	1/2 + 1/5	1/2 – 1/3
Levels 0–1	Not applicable.	Not applicable.
Level 2	Student: Make 1/2 and 1/5. 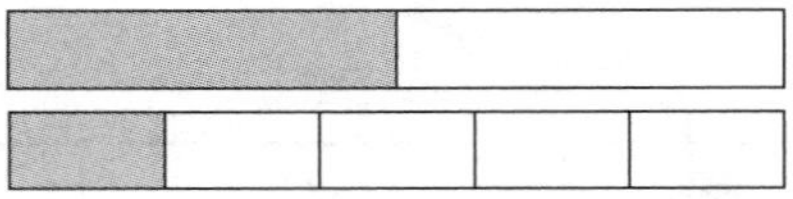 Student: That makes 2/7.	Student: Make 1/2 and 1/3. 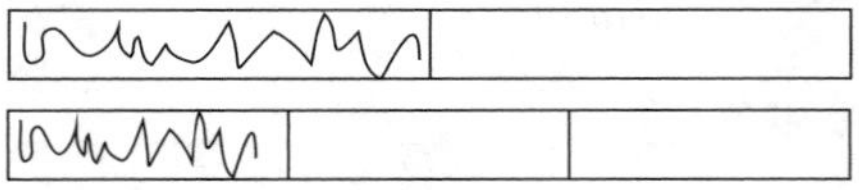 Student: When you take the 1/3 from the 1/2, you get this [erases 1/3 in the 1/2 strip], which is 1/3 [1 out of 3 parts is shaded]. 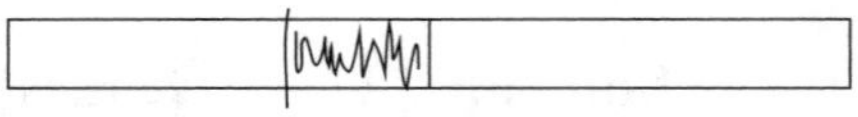
Level 3	Student: Make 1/2 and 1/5. 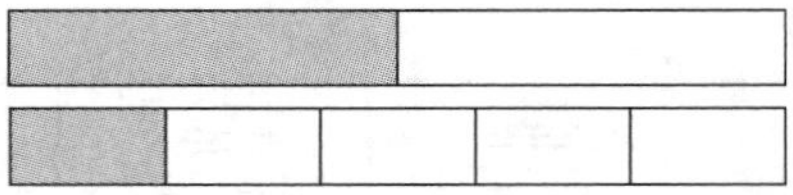 Student: That makes 2 out of 7 shaded parts. But the parts are not the same size, so I don't know what the fraction is.	Student: Make 1/2 and 1/3. 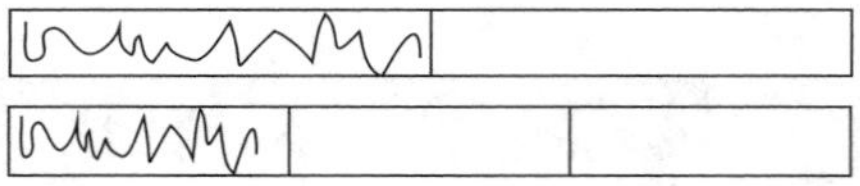 Student: When you take the 1/3 from the 1/2, you get this [erases 1/3 in the 1/2 strip]. 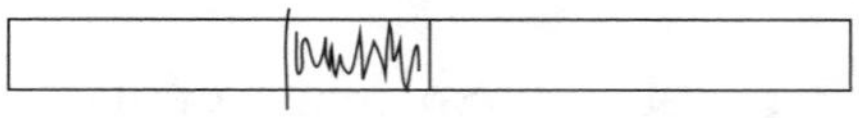 Student: That makes 1 out of 3 shaded parts. But the parts are not the same size, so I don't know what the fraction is.

Level 4	Students can do this problem if it is presented on an appropriate grid. Otherwise, they get stuck. Student: Make 1/2 and 1/5. Add the 1/5 to the 1/2. It looks like you get about 3 1/2 fifths.	Students can do this problem if it is presented on an appropriate grid. Otherwise, they get stuck. Student: Make 1/2 and 1/3. Student: Take the 1/3 from the 1/2, you get this [erases 1/3 in the 1/2 strip]. Sam: This looks like about 1/3 of 1/2.
Level 5	Student: First you make 1/2 and 1/5. Student: Then you make 1/2 and 1/5 into tenths, so the pieces are the same size. Student: Then you add the 1/5, which is 2/10, to 1/2, which makes 7/10. 	Student: First you make 1/2 and 1/3. Student: Then you make 1/2 and 1/3 into sixths, so the pieces are the same size. Student: Then you take away 1/3, which is 2/6, from 1/2, which is 1/6. Sam: So there's 1/6 left.
Level 6	Student draws a picture as in Level 5, and writes out the problem symbolically. $$\frac{1}{2} + \frac{1}{5} = \frac{5}{10} + \frac{2}{10} = \frac{7}{10}$$ **Teacher: Why does 10 work as a common denominator?** Response: Because when we did pictures for adding fractions, we always multiplied the denominators to find the common denominator.	Student draws a picture as in Level 5, and writes out the problem symbolically. $$\frac{1}{2} - \frac{1}{3} = \frac{3}{6} - \frac{2}{6} = \frac{1}{6}$$ **Teacher: Why does 6 work as a common denominator?** Response: Because when we did pictures for subtracting fractions, we always multiplied the denominators to find the common denominator.

Level 7	Student draws a picture as in Level 5, and writes out the problem symbolically. $$\frac{1}{2} + \frac{1}{5} = \frac{5}{10} + \frac{2}{10} = \frac{7}{10}$$ **Teacher: Why does 10 work as a common denominator?** Response: Because 2 and 5 both divide 10 equally so the pieces for halves and fifths can both be made from the pieces for tenths. See [pointing to picture] 1 fifth piece equals 2 tenth pieces and 1 half piece equals 5 tenth pieces.	Student draws a picture as in Level 5, and writes out the problem symbolically. $$\frac{1}{2} - \frac{1}{3} = \frac{3}{6} - \frac{2}{6} = \frac{1}{6}$$ **Teacher: Why does 6 work as a common denominator?** Response: Because 2 and 3 both divide 6 equally so the pieces for halves and thirds can both be made from the pieces for sixths. See [pointing to picture] 1 third piece equals 2 sixth pieces and 1 half piece equals 3 sixth pieces.

Draw rectangles on the dot paper to show how to solve the problems. Give the answer to each problem and explain why your picture shows that answer. If you can, show how to solve the problem symbolically.

	1/2 × 1/4	1/2 ÷ 1/3
Levels 0–1	Not applicable.	Not applicable.
Level 2	Student: Draws 1/2 and 1/4 and combines them, getting 2/6. 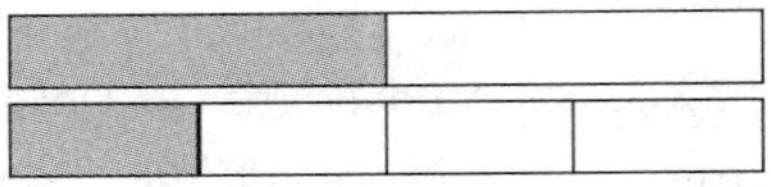	Student: Draws 1/2 and 1/3 and combines them, getting 2/5. 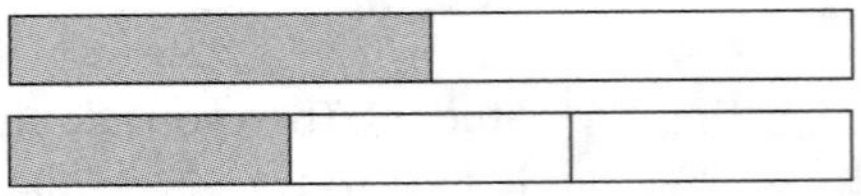
Level 3	Student: Shades 1/2 a rectangle horizontally, then 1/4 of the rectangle vertically. Says that 5/8 of the rectangle is shaded. 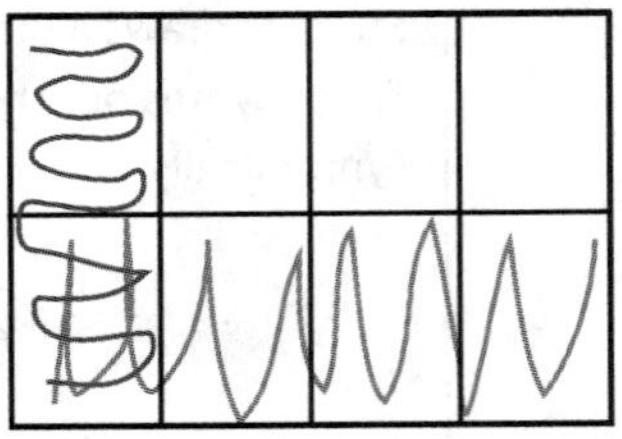	Student: Shades 1/2 a rectangle horizontally, then divides the shaded part into 4 equal pieces. Teacher: "How many fourths in 1/2?" Says there are 4 fourths in 1/2 and gives 4 as the answer. 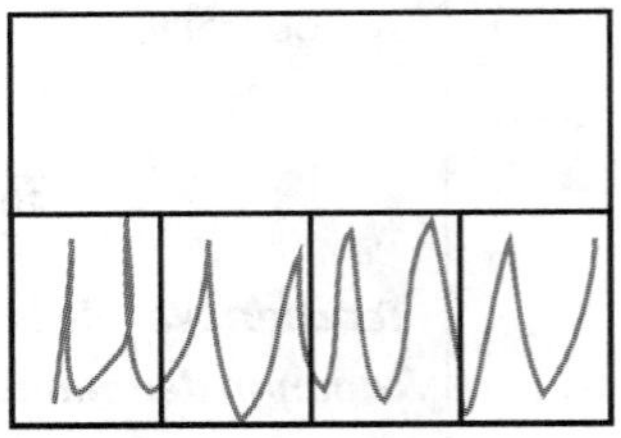

Level 4	Student: *[Shades 1/2 a rectangle horizontally.]* Take 1/4 of the 1/2 vertically—divide it into 4 equal pieces, shade one piece. I'd say this is 1/8 because there are 4 pieces on the bottom, so there would be 4 on the top. 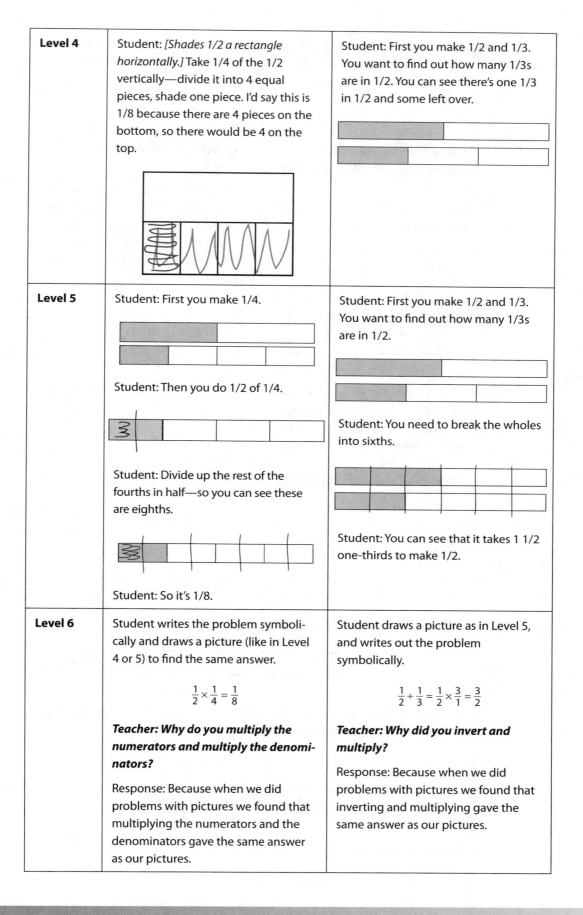	Student: First you make 1/2 and 1/3. You want to find out how many 1/3s are in 1/2. You can see there's one 1/3 in 1/2 and some left over.
Level 5	Student: First you make 1/4. Student: Then you do 1/2 of 1/4. Student: Divide up the rest of the fourths in half—so you can see these are eighths. Student: So it's 1/8.	Student: First you make 1/2 and 1/3. You want to find out how many 1/3s are in 1/2. Student: You need to break the wholes into sixths. Student: You can see that it takes 1 1/2 one-thirds to make 1/2.
Level 6	Student writes the problem symbolically and draws a picture (like in Level 4 or 5) to find the same answer. $$\frac{1}{2} \times \frac{1}{4} = \frac{1}{8}$$ ***Teacher: Why do you multiply the numerators and multiply the denominators?*** Response: Because when we did problems with pictures we found that multiplying the numerators and the denominators gave the same answer as our pictures.	Student draws a picture as in Level 5, and writes out the problem symbolically. $$\frac{1}{2} \div \frac{1}{3} = \frac{1}{2} \times \frac{3}{1} = \frac{3}{2}$$ ***Teacher: Why did you invert and multiply?*** Response: Because when we did problems with pictures we found that inverting and multiplying gave the same answer as our pictures.

Level 7	Student writes the problem symbolically and draws a picture (like in Level 4 or 5) to find the same answer.	Student draws a picture as in Level 5, and writes out the problem symbolically.
	$$\frac{1}{2} \times \frac{1}{4} = \frac{1}{8}$$	$$\frac{1}{2} \div \frac{1}{3} = \frac{1}{2} \times \frac{3}{1} = \frac{3}{2}$$
	Teacher: Why do you multiply the numerators and multiply the denominators?	***Teacher: Why did you invert and multiply?***
	Response: *[Draws the picture below, if it was not already drawn.]*	Response: Well, we want to know how many thirds are in 1/2. One way to do this problem is to find out how many thirds are in 1 (which is 3) and take half of that. So we get a multiplication problem.
	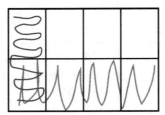	
	The 2 rows show 1/2; the 4 columns show 1/4. So there are 8 little rectangles—that makes eighths. The part that is double shaded is 1/8—its 1 because there is 1 half and 1 fourth.	$$\frac{1}{2} \times 3 = \frac{1}{2} \times \frac{3}{1}$$

Use pictures to find the following. If you can, show how to solve the problem symbolically.

	2 ÷ 5
Levels 0–2	Not applicable.
Level 3	Student: First cut the cakes into fourths and give one to each of 5 people. Student: Then divide up the leftover pieces into fourths. Each person gets 2 of these pieces. We'll just leave the extras out. Student: So each person gets 1/4 + 1/4 + 1/4. *[The small pieces are really 1/16 not 1/4.]*

Level 4	Student: First cut the cakes into fourths and give one to each person.

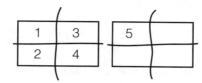

Student: Then divide up the leftover pieces into fourths. Each person gets 2 of these pieces, which you can see from the picture are really sixteenths of the cake. And 1/4 is 4/16. We'll just leave the extras out.

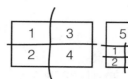

Student: So each person gets 4/16 + 1/16 + 1/16 = 6/16. *[Student missed the 2 empty small pieces. The splitting-in-half strategy won't work for this problem, no matter how small you make the pieces.]*

Level 5	Student: You want to divide 2 cakes equally between 5 kids. So divide each cake into 5 pieces.

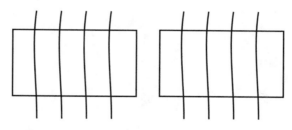

Student: One person would get one piece from each cake.

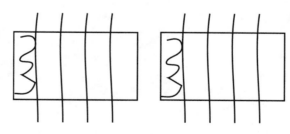

Student: So each person gets 2/5 of a cake.

| Level 6 | Student writes the problem symbolically and draws a picture (like in Level 5) to find the same answer.

$$2 \div 5 = \frac{2}{1} \div \frac{5}{1} = \frac{2}{1} \times \frac{1}{5} = \frac{2}{5}$$

Teacher: Why did you invert and multiply?

Response: Because when we did problems with pictures we found that inverting and multiplying gave the same answer as our pictures. |
|---|---|
| Level 7 | Student writes the problem symbolically and draws a picture (like in Level 5) to find the same answer.

$$2 \div 5 = \frac{2}{1} \div \frac{5}{1} = \frac{2}{1} \times \frac{1}{5} = \frac{2}{5}$$

Teacher: Why did you invert and multiply?

Response: *[Pointing to the same picture as shown in Level 5]* Divide each 1 in 2 into 5 equal parts. We get 1/5 from each 1. Because there are 2 ones in 2, we get 2 fifths, which is the multiplication problem $2 \times \frac{1}{5} = \frac{2}{5}$. |

Glossary

NUMERATOR/DENOMINATOR

In the fraction a/b, *a* is the *numerator*, and *b* is the *denominator*.

UNIT AND NON-UNIT FRACTIONS

A *unit fraction* is a fraction in which the numerator is 1.

A *non-unit fraction* has a numerator not equal to 1 or 0.

PROPER AND IMPROPER FRACTIONS, MIXED NUMBERS

A *proper fraction* is a fraction in which the numerator is less than or equal to the denominator (e.g., 5/6, 3/3).

An *improper fraction* is a fraction in which the numerator is greater than the denominator (e.g., 6/5).

A *mixed number* has both a whole number and a fractional part (e.g., 3 4/5).

COMMON DENOMINATORS

Two fractions have a *common denominator* if their denominators are equal (e.g., 2/7 and 4/7).

RECIPROCAL

The *reciprocal* (or multiplicative inverse) of a fraction c/d is the fraction d/c because $\frac{c}{d} \cdot \frac{d}{c} = 1$ (e.g., 3/5 and 5/3 are reciprocals of each other).

DECIMAL FRACTIONS

Decimal fractions have powers of ten as denominators. So 3/10, 4/100, 35/1000 are all decimal fractions. Decimal fractions are special because they can also be expressed as decimals. For example: 3/10 = .3.

References

Ball, D. L. 1993. "Halves, Pieces, and Twoths: Constructing Representational Contexts in Teaching Fractions." In T. Carpenter, E. Fennema, & T. Romberg, (Eds.), *Rational Numbers: An Integration of Research*. Hillsdale, NJ: Erlbaum, pp. 157–196.

Baroody, A. J., & Ginsburg, H. P. 1990. "Children's Learning: A Cognitive View." In R. B. Davis, C. A. Maher, & N. Noddings (Eds.), "Constructivist Views on the Teaching and Learning of Mathematics." *Journal for Research in Mathematics Education Monograph Number 4*. Reston, VA: National Council of Teachers of Mathematics, pp. 51–64.

Battista, M. T. 1999. "The Mathematical Miseducation of America's Youth: Ignoring Research and Scientific Study in Education." *Phi Delta Kappan* 80(6): 424–433.

Battista, M. T. 2001. "How Do Children Learn Mathematics? Research and Reform in Mathematics Education." In Thomas Loveless (Ed.), *The Great Curriculum Debate: How Should We Teach Reading and Math?* Washington, DC: Brookings Press, pp. 42–84. (Based on a paper presented at the conference, "Curriculum Wars: Alternative Approaches to Reading and Mathematics." Harvard University, October 21–22, 1999.)

Battista, M. T. (2004). "Applying Cognition-Based Assessment to Elementary School Students' Development of Understanding of Area and Volume Measurement." *Mathematical Thinking and Learning* 6(2): 185–204.

Battista, M. T., & Clements, D. H. 1996. "Students' Understanding of Three-Dimensional Rectangular Arrays of Cubes." *Journal for Research in Mathematics Education* 27(3): 258–292.

Battista, M. T., Clements, D. H., Arnoff, J., Battista, K., & Borrow, C.V.A. 1998. Students' Spatial Structuring and Enumeration of 2D Arrays of Squares." *Journal for Research in Mathematics Education* 29(5): 503–532.

Black, P., & Wiliam, D. 1998. "Raising Standards Through Classroom Assessment." *Phi Delta Kappan* 80(2): 139–148.

Bransford, J. D., Brown, A. L., & Cocking, R. R. 1999. *How People Learn: Brain, Mind, Experience, and School*. Washington, DC: National Research Council.

Buschman, Larry. 2001. "Using Student Interviews to Guide Classroom Instruction: An Action Research Project." *Teaching Children Mathematics* (December): 222–227.

Carpenter, T. P., & Fennema, E. 1991. "Research and Cognitively Guided Instruction." In E. Fennema, T. P. Carpenter, & S. J. Lamon (Eds.), *Integrating Research on Teaching and Learning Mathematics*. Albany: State University of New York Press, pp. 1–16.

Carpenter, T. P., Franke, M. L., Jacobs, V. R., Fennema, E., & Empson, S. B. 1998. "A Longitudinal Study of Invention and Understanding in Children's Multidigit Addition and Subtraction." *Journal for Research in Mathematics Education* 29(1): 3–20.

Cobb, P., & Wheatley, G. 1988. "Children's Initial Understanding of Ten." *Focus on Learning Problems in Mathematics* 10(3): 1–28.

Cobb, P., Wood, T., Yackel, E., Nicholls, J., Wheatley, G., Trigatti, B., & Perlwitz, M. 1991. "Assessment of a Problem-Centered Second-Grade Mathematics Project." *Journal for Research in Mathematics Education* 22(1): 3–29.

De Corte, E., Greer, B., & Verschaffel, L. 1996. "Mathematics Teaching and Learning." In D. C. Berliner & R. C. Calfee (Eds.), *Handbook of Educational Psychology*. New York: Simon & Schuster Macmillan, pp. 491–549.

Fennema, E., Carpenter, T. P., Franke, M. L., Levi, L., Jacobs, V. R., & Empson, S. B. 1996. "A Longitudinal Study of Learning to Use Children's Thinking in Mathematics Instruction." *Journal for Research in Mathematics Education* 27(4): 403–434.

Fennema, E., & Franke, M. L. 1992. "Teachers' Knowledge and Its Impact." In D. A. Grouws (Ed.), *Handbook of Research on Mathematics Teaching*. Reston, VA: National Council of Teachers of Mathematics/Macmillan, pp. 127–164.

Fuson, K. C., Wearne, D., Hiebert, J. C., Murray, H. G., Human, P. G., Olivier, A. L., et al. 1997. "Children's Conceptual Structures for Multidigit Numbers and Methods of Multidigit Addition and Subtraction." *Journal for Research in Mathematics Education* 28(2): 130–162.

Greeno, J. G., Collins, A. M., & Resnick, L. 1996. "Cognition and Learning." In D. C. Berliner & R. C. Calfee (Eds.), *Handbook of Educational Psychology*. New York: Simon & Schuster Macmillan, pp. 15–46.

Hiebert, J., & Carpenter, T. P. 1992. "Learning and Teaching with Understanding." In D. A. Grouws (Ed.), *Handbook of Research on Mathematics Teaching*. Reston, VA: National Council of Teachers of Mathematics/Macmillan, pp. 65–97.

Lester, F. K. 1994. "Musing About Mathematical Problem-Solving Research: 1970–1994." *Journal for Research in Mathematics Education* 25(6): 660–675.

National Research Council. 1989. *Everybody Counts*. Washington, DC: National Academy Press.

Olive, J., & Steffe, L. P. 2002. "The Construction of an Iterative Fractional Scheme: The Case of Joe." *Mathematical Behavior* 20: 413–437.

Prawat, R. S. 1999. "Dewey, Peirce, and the Learning Paradox." *American Educational Research Journal* 36(1): 47–76.

Romberg, T. A. 1992. "Further Thoughts on the Standards: A Reaction to Apple." *Journal for Research in Mathematics Education* 23(5): 432–437.

Saxe, G. et al. 2007. "Learning About Fractions as Points on a Number Line." *The Learning of Mathematics: NCTM 2007 Yearbook*, 221–238.

Schoenfeld, A. C. 1994. "What Do We Know About Mathematics Curricula." *Journal of Mathematical Behavior* 13: 55–80.

Steffe, L. P. 1988. "Children's Construction of Number Sequences and Multiplying Schemes." In J. Hiebert & M. Behr (Eds.), *Number Concepts and Operations in the Middle Grades*. Reston, VA: National Council of Teachers of Mathematics, pp. 119–140.

Steffe, L. P. 1992. "Schemes of Action and Operation Involving Composite Units." *Learning and Individual Differences* 4(3): 259–309.

Steffe, L. P., & D'Ambrosio, B. S. 1995. "Toward a Working Model of Constructivist Teaching: A Reaction to Simon." *Journal for Research in Mathematics Education* 26(2): 146–159.

Steffe, L. P., & Kieren, T. 1994. "Radical Constructivism and Mathematics Education." *Journal for Research in Mathematics Education* 25(6): 711–733.

Tierney, C., Ogonowski, M., Rubin, A., & Russell, S. J. 1996. *Different Shapes, Equal Pieces: Fractions and Area (Investigations in Number, Data, and Space, Grade 4)*. Glenview, IL: Scott-Foresman.

van Hiele, P. M. 1986. *Structure and Insight*. Orlando: Academic Press.

von Glasersfeld, Ernst. 1995. *Radical Constructivism: A Way of Knowing and Learning*. Washington, DC: Falmer Press.